Little Mix

OUR WORLD

MICHAEL JOSEPH
an imprint of
PENGUIN BOOKS

MICHAEL JOSEPH

UK | USA | Canada | Ireland | Australia
India | New Zealand | South Africa

Michael Joseph is part of the Penguin Random House group of companies
whose addresses can be found at global.penguinrandomhouse.com

Penguin
Random House
UK

First published in 2016
001

Designed and typeset by Smith and Gilmour Ltd
Printed and bound by Firmengruppe APPL, aprinta druck, Wemding, Germany
Colour reproduction by Altaimage Ltd

A CIP catalogue record for this book is available from the British Library

ISBN: 978–1–405–92742–0

MIX
Paper from
responsible sources
FSC® C018179

Penguin Random House is committed to a
sustainable future for our business, our readers
and our planet. This book is made from Forest
Stewardship Council® certified paper.

CONTENTS

INTRODUCTION

Sitting down to write this book took us back to how it all began, in 2011, before anyone had even thought of Little Mix. We didn't know each other but all any of us wanted was to sing and perform. At the same time, the idea of being pop stars seemed massively out of reach. Luckily for us, our families believed in us and gave us the push we needed to chase the dream we shared.

We'll always be thankful.

None of us dared to think we could go all the way on *The X Factor*. It's not the kind of thing that happens to normal girls like us ... Little did we know!

We not only succeeded, we made history as the first group ever to win the show. Looking back, we all believe that fate, or destiny, or whatever you want to call it, was on our side. Right people, right place, right time. From the word go, it was as if Little Mix was meant to be and as soon as we got put into a group together things began to fall into place. We realized we all had the same vision.

Once we found each other, we found our voice.

At the heart of everything we've achieved so far is our unbreakable friendship. We don't even know how to find the words for how close we are. We're family – four sisters who'd do anything for each other.

In so many ways our lives have changed beyond anything we knew before, yet we're still the same four girls who auditioned for *The X Factor*. Sometimes we look at each other and go: 'This is *insane*!'

Knowing that so many of you relate to our music means so much. For us, being on stage and seeing thousands of people sing the words to our songs is the most magical feeling. We're lucky to have the best fans ever – there for us, and each other. We can't thank you enough for your love and support, for making this whole experience so incredible.

More than anything, we hope our story will inspire you to chase your dreams – even when they seem impossible. We know how that feels and we're proof it *can* be done. As long as you give your best, put in the hard graft and never stop believing, you really can change your life.

Go for it!

Jeme ♥ x

Leigh xx x

Jade x

Lesy ♥

the Beginning

Jade

DOB:
26 DECEMBER 1992

IN THREE WORDS:
THOUGHTFUL, PECULIAR, LOVING

MOST LIKELY TO SAY:
'ANYONE CAN ACHIEVE THEIR
DREAMS IF THEY HAVE THE
COURAGE TO PURSUE THEM.'

Growing up, it was me, my mam and dad, and my big brother, Karl. We were working class, what I'd call a typical normal family, living in a terraced house in a little cul-de-sac in South Shields, in the North East. My dad, Jimmy, is a taxi driver and, when I was little, my mam, Norma, worked as the business manager at the school I went to. I absolutely loved primary school and with my mam being around I couldn't go wrong. My brother's five years older and I idolized him. I still do! I always wanted to be like him so everything he did, I copied. If he was into a certain type of music, so was I. If he played football, I wanted to too. I'd go with my mam to watch him play every weekend, cheering him on. I worshipped him. I was quite tomboyish as a child, but was also into tap and ballet. It was a really lovely childhood.

When I got to secondary school things changed. All my friends went to a different school so I was on my own with no mates. I was a bit of a swot, painfully shy, and didn't stand a chance really. I got bullied quite badly. I'd get picked on by the popular gang and there was this one girl who really had it in for me. She was in my year but she was a big girl and would push me around and tell me I was ugly. This particular girl used to corner me in the toilets, shout things like 'P***' and throw bleach powder at me – once she got her mates to hold me down and drew a bindi on my forehead. They would point and laugh. I'd never experienced racism or prejudice before then. I had no one to talk to about it so it got to the point where I wasn't really going into school, or I'd turn up and hide in the toilets or in my drama teacher's classroom and stay there all day, waiting for the bell to go, then I'd run. What was weird was that outside school I was quite confident, going to drama and dance classes and singing in musicals and stuff, but at school I was an absolute mess. Just walking into the building would fill me with dread.

Eventually, my mam found out what was going on, stormed into school and told the head of year to sort it out. I was mortified, not wanting anyone to know, thinking I'd be even more uncool. The school suspended the girl who was bullying me, then she got moved to another class and from then on things got better. A girl called Ruth was told to chaperone me and that's how I got to know her best friend, Holly. To start with Holly hated it because she was lumbered with the geek, taking her friend away from her, but as time went on we became close and we've been best friends ever

> SHE WAS A BIG GIRL AND WOULD PUSH ME AROUND AND TELL ME I WAS UGLY . . . I'D NEVER EXPERIENCED RACISM OR PREJUDICE BEFORE THEN.

since. We look back now and find the whole situation hilarious, especially since we're so inseparable now. My other best friend, Anna, I used to sing with. She moved to my school in Year 8 and thankfully I then had a few friends around me.

I was about thirteen when I got anorexia. I think it was the culmination of a lot of stuff, not just the bullying. My mam and dad were arguing a lot and my Granda Mohammed, who I was really close to, died. He was everything to me, the nicest man ever, and so calming to be around. He lived at the bottom of our road, so I'd always be round there, every day. Then he got ill and went into hospital. A couple of weeks later he died of heart failure. I'd been in to see him and, looking back, it was as if he knew what was coming because when I was leaving he kissed me on the forehead and said, 'Look after yourself. I love you.' It seemed weird. I said, 'I love you, Granda,' thinking I'd see him the next day, and left. That night he died.

It was the first time I'd lost anyone I loved and I found it really hard to deal with.

At thirteen, you're at that age when you don't really have control over anything and I felt as if the only thing I could control was what I was eating. I started skipping meals and stuff like that. I would look in the mirror and it wasn't that I'd think I was fat, I just had it in my head that I wanted to be really, really skinny. I used to find out what foods would work as a laxative and that's what I'd eat, if I was going to eat, or I'd take ages over a plate of food, have minuscule amounts on my fork and, when no one was looking, I'd hide it or throw it in the bin.

For a good couple of years nobody really knew what was going on because I wore baggy clothes and

I SAID, 'I LOVE YOU, GRANDA,' THINKING I'D SEE HIM THE NEXT DAY, AND LEFT. THAT NIGHT HE DIED.

IN YEAR 9 I SANG
IN ASSEMBLY AND
PEOPLE WERE
GOING, 'OH, SHE
CAN SING!'

Mam took me to Australia to see family there for a few weeks, which was nice. It was like a retreat, a chance to get away from everything and sort my head out a bit. When I got back we got proper help, and I started going to a clinic for eating disorders in Sunderland. My weight had dropped to around six stone by then. It took going to hospital to make me realize what I was actually doing, that it wasn't a game, it was something really serious. They sat me down in the clinic and were quite tough at first, spelling it out: 'You're destroying your body and if you keep doing this you will die.'

It wasn't easy to turn things round and I was stubborn to start with but I had a friend going through the same thing, only much worse than me, and she ended up in hospital, in a specialist unit, in a bad way. I went to see her and she was so ill; her poor parents were devastated. I thought, 'Fucking hell, I can't do this to my family.' It shocked me into making a change.

From then on I went to hospital every week as an out-patient and they weighed me to see how I was doing. There was always the threat of being admitted if my weight dropped to a certain level. I hated the staff at first but as time went by I loved them for helping me. I had therapy sessions, and my mam got help as well with how best to react if I didn't want to eat, what kind of meals to cook for me, all that kind of thing. Everyone always had an eye on me to make sure I was eating.

Towards the end of secondary school things picked up for me and I didn't care as much if I was in the popular gang or not. I had a good core group of friends who were there for me and that was all that mattered. I was singing a lot outside of school, and in Year 9 I sang in assembly and people were going, 'Oh, she can sing!' In 2008, when I was fifteen, I did *The X Factor* for the first time and got as far as Boot Camp, and I think that helped give me a bit of street cred and a confidence boost at the same time.

It took a couple of years to recover from anorexia but I gradually got better and just before I went in for *The X Factor* in 2011 I was discharged from hospital.

I feel I was very lucky to get help before things had spiralled too much out of control. Now, when I look back, I can't believe I did that to my family and friends, and to myself. I'm so grateful to everyone around me at that time, who had the patience and love to help me through it all, and so sorry that I behaved so badly to them. I would never, ever, get myself in that situation again. Lots of young people go through anorexia and not enough of them talk about it. I'd hate for anyone to think that because I went through it, it's OK. It's not. I want people to know they can get help, like I did, and that there is a way to get better.

Jesy

DOB:
14 JUNE 1991

IN THREE WORDS:
STRONG, WEIRD, CARING

MOST LIKELY TO SAY:
'BE YOURSELF AND NEVER TRY TO
CHANGE WHO YOU ARE. EVERYONE
IS DIFFERENT AND IF WE ALL
LOOKED THE SAME, THE WORLD
WOULD BE BORING.'

I've got two brothers and a sister and home was a bit of a madhouse when I was growing up. We're all quite close in age. My sister, Jade, is the eldest, five years older than me. My big brother, Johnny, is a couple of years older than me, and there's a year or so between me and my younger brother, Joe.

I grew up in Essex and when I was young we moved around a lot. We actually lived in twelve different houses, and we went to Cornwall for a little while. I never minded moving; it was exciting to me, especially the time we spent in Cornwall. We went there because my mum, Janis, loved it and had always wanted to live in that part of the world.

It was so beautiful. We were right next to the sea and could go to the beach every day. The house was bigger than what we were used to – it felt like a mansion to us. It had a huge winding staircase and when Mum was out we'd go down it on mattresses! We'd only been in Cornwall about six months when my brothers got trials for West Ham and we moved again, to Hornchurch, in Essex. I was about nine or ten, I think. My brothers were quite naughty, typical boys I suppose, fighting all the time, which caused so much grief. They're good boys now. My sister and me were quite good but we argued all the time too. Funny how things change, because now we're all really close and protective of each other. I love my family so much. They're amazing.

My mum brought us up on her own. Thanks to her, I've got good morals – not because she was strict with us, more because she set such a good example. She never got any money or anything from my dad, so how she managed with four kids I have no idea. I know for a fact it was a struggle, very stressful for her, but I was so young I wasn't really aware of what was going on or how tough things were. Somehow she did a great job and I never felt I was missing out on anything. Everything she had to deal with could have got her down, but she's a survivor and if you met her, you'd never imagine she'd been through half the stuff she has. She's so lovely and kind-hearted, not a bad bone in her body. I think it's incredible how strong she is. All her life she's worked hard, doing loads of jobs to earn as much money as possible for us. She's been a paramedic, a firefighter, a barmaid, and now she's a police community support officer.

TO ME, SHE'S WONDER WOMAN.

I was always an eccentric little girl, doing accents and silly voices, and was into performing and drama when I was quite young. I don't really know where that came from, probably my mum. When she was younger she was a cover girl on *Jackie* magazine and did adverts and theatre work, but I never had any sense of her pushing me to perform, although she always gave me lots of encouragement and support. On Saturdays I went to a theatre school to do drama, dancing and singing, and I loved it. From there I joined an agency and got into acting, which was always my main passion. I was probably about eight when I had my first audition, for a film called *Man on Fire*. I was up for the main part of the little girl opposite Denzel Washington, who's my favourite actor now. I remember my mum taking me to London to audition, and my agent saying I had to do an American accent and get it absolutely spot on. I knew it was a big deal, but I was so young I don't think I understood how huge it was. For my audition I had to read a prayer and did well enough to keep getting called back until I was down to the last four, but there was this one word in the script I couldn't get right. I can't remember what it was now but every time I said it, it came out sounding British. They got me to do it over and over but I couldn't quite get the American accent. The part went to Dakota Fanning and it was only when I saw the film and recognized the scene I'd done for my audition that I realized how massive the role was. I can't imagine what I'd be doing now if I'd got it.

I did a few adverts, one for Hula Hoops that got used on TV in Germany. When I auditioned for that all I had to do was scream as loud as I could, and cry. I never saw how

> ## I WAS ALWAYS AN ECCENTRIC LITTLE GIRL, DOING ACCENTS AND SILLY VOICES.

the finished ad turned out. I played a little scientist on a CBBC programme and was an extra in a few films. I was in the ballroom scene in *Harry Potter and the Goblet of Fire*, and the Hugh Grant film *About a Boy*. I spent five weeks filming scenes for *The Others*, with Nicole Kidman, but they never got used.

When I was twelve I auditioned for a scholarship at the Sylvia Young Theatre School, in London, and got down to the last three. Looking back, what's weird is that one of the boys I was up against was my best friend there, and he's now best friends with my fiancé, Jake. Even though I loved Sylvia Young's, I never really felt like I fitted in. It was quite cliquey and everyone had to be a certain way. We all had elocution lessons, which meant everybody sounded the same. I've got a strong Essex accent but while I was there I sounded really posh, which wasn't me at all. The drama and that side of things was great but there were classes I didn't enjoy, like ballet, and I'd skip some days, which wasn't fair on my mum when the fees were so expensive.

After eighteen months I left and went to a normal secondary school in Upminster, and it was such a shock. At Sylvia Young's there was only one class of twenty-five people in my whole year, whereas in my new school there were so many kids, and I didn't know anyone and found it really daunting. I was the new girl, the latecomer, and there were some awful bitchy girls who started bullying me – calling me names, saying nasty things about how I looked, and threatening to wait for me after school and kick my head in. I was about thirteen, with no friends at the school, and it was a horrible time. The girls who were picking on me got a lad they knew, a couple of years older in Year 11, to

I WAS THE
NEW GIRL, THE
LATECOMER, AND
THERE WERE SOME
AWFUL BITCHY
GIRLS WHO STARTED
BULLYING ME.

push me around. He bullied me really badly. I was going home in tears, hating it, and got to the point where I was so scared I didn't want to go to school. My mum was in a predicament. She didn't want to make me go when I was having such a bad time but the authorities were strict about attendance and parents were being taken to court. You could go to prison if your kid didn't go to school. I was bullied every day for months and got so stressed and upset I got alopecia and my hair started falling out. My skin flared up with a condition called rosacea that spread all over my face and made it red and inflamed. It looked awful, like bad acne, and there was nothing I could do about it because we weren't allowed to wear make-up in school. I know some people think name-calling isn't the worst thing kids can experience but when you're getting it every day it takes hold, especially when you're in your teens and everything affects you so much. Even when I wasn't in school the abuse was still going round and round inside my head the whole time, making me feel worse. In the end, my sister went to the school and scared the shit out of the boy who was bullying me. He never came near me again and the girls left me alone as well.

> **I KNOW SOME PEOPLE THINK NAME-CALLING ISN'T THE WORST THING KIDS CAN EXPERIENCE BUT WHEN YOU'RE GETTING IT EVERY DAY IT TAKES HOLD.**

One of my teachers told me about a new school that was opening in Dagenham, specializing in drama and singing and dance, and said she'd be able to get me a place. I wasn't sure at first because I was worried about it being in a rough area. I also felt like I'd been in and out of schools and never settled anywhere but I decided to go for it and, in Year 9, started at Jo Richardson's, which I loved. My heart was in

Leigh-Anne

DOB:
4 OCTOBER 1991

IN THREE WORDS:
SILLY, SENSITIVE, FUN

MOST LIKELY TO SAY:
'YOU HAVE TO BELIEVE IN
YOURSELF BECAUSE IF YOU
DON'T, NO ONE ELSE WILL.'

I'm the baby, the youngest of three girls. Sairah is two years older and there's eight years between me and my eldest sister, Sian. When I was little we lived in a terraced house in High Wycombe and I shared a room with Sairah. I was super-shy growing up and only wanted to be with my mum and dad. My parents were always hard-working. My dad, John, had his own business fixing car axels, and my mum, Deborah, worked her way up to supermarket manager, then did a teacher-training course in her spare time. She went on to teach history, became head of year and then a child protection officer. I'm proud of what they achieved and the example they set for us.

When my dad was younger, he was a professional boxer, which I thought was amazingly cool. He gave it up when he broke his fist and I think it will always be one of his biggest regrets, because he really loved it. He's so talented and creative, super funny. He used to be an actor and did loads of plays, which is maybe where me wanting to be a performer comes from.

From the age of about nine I wanted to sing and on Sundays went to the Sylvia Young Theatre School, but I was so nervous I'd always be in the corner and had no stage presence. I went to Stagecoach as well and did lots of talent competitions. I was still so shy I would literally crumble as soon as I got on the stage.

When I was about twelve we moved to a bigger house with a bigger garden. There was a tiny box room, the smallest room you've ever seen, and that was my bedroom. There was no door, so I had one of those curtains made of dangly bits to give me a bit of privacy.

The early part of my childhood was lovely. I was very get-up-and-go and always wanted to be doing something. I had singing lessons, played different musical instruments, did piano for a year, and for a while I had a drum kit that ended up in the garage. I've no idea where it is now. It's annoying when I look back that I had so much opportunity but I didn't keep those things up – I don't know why.

My parents split up when I was about thirteen. Dad wasn't happy, Mum wasn't happy, and there was a lot of tension in the house. Towards the end they would sometimes fight and it was hard to witness all the arguing and shouting. I hated it. They were apart for about a year and then when my grandma died, my mum's mum, it brought them back

> I WENT TO STAGECOACH AS WELL AND DID LOTS OF TALENT COMPETITIONS. I WAS STILL SO SHY I WOULD LITERALLY CRUMBLE AS SOON AS I GOT ON THE STAGE.

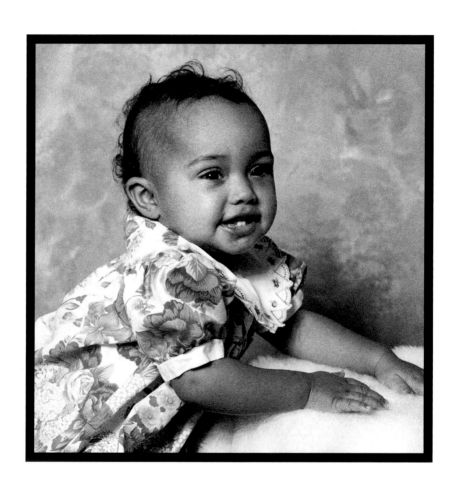

together. My dad supported Mum and that was beautiful, but they just weren't made for each other. I was about fourteen when they split up again. My sister Sairah stayed with Dad and I moved with my mum into a little flat down the road. The new place was lovely and I had a bigger room, and remember being excited about that. I think that was when me and Sairah started to get closer. Growing up, we were like cat and dog and at the time of the move we were in that teenage fighting stage. We had some bad fights. I would steal her best shoes and ruin them, and when I was fourteen or fifteen I remember taking her ID. She was so angry with me. It was good for us having our own space and not being on top of each other.

Once we moved I didn't see that much of my dad. I'd always been a proper daddy's girl when I was little, but as I got older I became closer to my mum. I regret not making more of an effort with my dad because while both my parents were supportive, Dad was the creative one who pushed me to go to stage school so I could do performing arts. He was always the one who said I could be a singer if that's what I really wanted, whereas Mum wanted me to go to uni. I know my dad did everything in his power to make sure we had it all and I so wish I'd made more of a fuss of him back then.

I wouldn't say I was a goody two-shoes at school but I was hard-working, always wanting to do my best. I was never part of the cool crowd. In Year 7, me and my friends used to look at another group of girls in my year and wish we were more like them, they were so hot, but from Year 9 on we really found ourselves and felt we didn't need to be a certain way; we were cool just being ourselves. I'm the luckiest girl when it comes to my friends. We were solid and never argued or fell out.

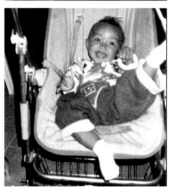

[DAD] WAS ALWAYS THE ONE WHO SAID I COULD BE A SINGER IF THAT'S WHAT I REALLY WANTED.

A Little Dream, A Lot of Love

| A LITTLE DREAM, A LOT OF LOVE

PERRIE: Before I met the girls at Boot Camp in August 2011, I found the *X Factor* experience very lonely. Everyone seemed so confident and cocky and they all seemed to be friends. I didn't know anybody and just sat by myself. I found Boot Camp nerve-racking, really scary. I didn't like the atmosphere; it was too competitive. You couldn't walk down the corridor without hearing people singing the whole time. They couldn't wait to be on camera, whereas I hated it when the camera came round. I didn't have any confidence and was panicking, ringing my mam every night, saying I wanted to go home, begging her to come and pick me up. She couldn't understand, but I just didn't like it.

They got us all in a room and the judges and producers were weighing everyone up, looking to put people into groups, trying to work out who would go well together. I was in the corner watching it happen, feeling that I didn't look right. They kept getting me to move and stand with different people, but it was obvious wherever they put me it wasn't working. They'd go, 'Can you stand here? Can you move over there? Where does she fit?'

I DIDN'T FIT ANYWHERE.

I remember seeing Jesy and thinking she was very out there with her outfit, very street, with this crazy big hair. I thought she was so cool. When I got put in a group with her all of a sudden I had someone to talk to and didn't feel so alone. She was the first person I got close to. I remember our group were sat on the stairs, going, 'Right, what're we

going to do?' and Jesy saying we should all sing so we knew what we sounded like, and go from there. I was panicking, thinking, 'Oh god, I don't want to sing in front of them,' but when I did Jesy said I'd blown her away, I wasn't what she expected, and that really boosted my confidence. I decided I had to stop being such a wimp, and that was when I started enjoying it and got a taste for what it would be like to do well. I thought, 'I can do this if I try,' and really came out of my shell.

We were practising our harmonies for Destiny's Child's 'Survivor' when Elliot Kennedy, who was talent coaching on the show, heard us. He came in and wanted to know who was singing the high harmony. I told him it was me and he chatted for a bit, said he was liking our sound and left us rehearsing. Later he told me he had run straight to the producers and told them he'd just heard someone with an insane voice. Apparently by then they already had a list of people they wanted for the groups and my name wasn't on it. I'd always been so nervous that they'd never heard me sing well, so if it hadn't been for Elliot going past when he did, I wouldn't have been put through.

Everything happens for a reason.

Jesy was sharing with Leigh-Anne, and she introduced us. I remember being in their room eating pizza and having girly chats with Jesy while Leigh-Anne was in bed trying to sleep and she was so nice, didn't mind us talking, keeping her awake. I thought she was the sweetest girl ever. I'd been told there was another girl there from South Shields. Someone in my street was friends with Jade's mam and said to look out for her. One day I was sat next to a girl

EVERYTHING HAPPENS FOR A REASON.

and somehow I knew it was her. It was so weird. I said, 'Are you Jade?' We clicked straight away.

JESY ⁑ I'm the biggest fan of *The X Factor* and when I met Jade at Boot Camp I recognized her from when she'd auditioned years before. I thought she was so cute, the prettiest little thing I'd ever seen. We automatically became friends. It sounds really bad but to start with I couldn't understand a word she said because her North East accent was so strong!

When I got to my room I was dreading it, hoping they hadn't put me with one of the crazy people you get on the show. I walked in, saw Leigh-Anne and we clicked straight away. She was lovely. The conversation flowed and we talked about our ex boyfriends. It was like we'd known each other forever. I thought she was so pretty, really sweet. The first Boot Camp challenge was learning a song you'd been given and performing it in front of the judges. Me and Leigh-Anne were up all night working on our song, talking, really excited, and in the morning, doing our hair in front of the mirror, we looked at each other and it was like, 'We look good together.' We decided to stick together in case it didn't work out for us as solo artists, hoping they'd put us in a group. Later in the day I saw Jade and introduced her to Leigh-Anne. I think the producers clocked the three of us, and it planted a seed, and they put us with another girl in a group called Orion. That was great but then I got taken out and put in a different group, Faux Pas, with Perrie. I remember thinking she was sweet, a little hippy, but that it didn't suit me being in a group with her – we looked too different. Perrie reminded me of Diana Vickers and I expected her to

I THOUGHT [JADE] WAS SO CUTE, THE PRETTIEST LITTLE THING I'D EVER SEEN.

sound like her then when she sang – *oh my god!* – she was a proper soul singer, insane. I was so shocked – and so thankful to be in a group with her! I thought, 'You're the key!'

LEIGH-ANNE : I remember seeing Jesy across the room at my first audition at the O2 and thinking, 'That girl looks sick, so cool.' When I got to Boot Camp I saw I was sharing a room with her. We stayed up all night talking about our exes and we clicked straight away. Boot Camp is a scary situation and it was so lovely to be able to connect and be friends with someone. I remember one day me and Jesy were sitting doing our hair, looking in the mirror, thinking we looked good together. Jesy introduced me to Jade and the three of us stuck together, hoping that if they put people into groups they'd see us as a three, which was what happened. I thought Jade was really sweet, very quiet, then when we started working together I saw she was so talented. She did all our harmonies and was amazing. When Jesy got taken out of our group and put in another one with Perrie we were so upset because we'd got close and all of a sudden it felt like we were competing with each other. It never got awkward between us though, and I remember Jesy liked Perrie straight away and sang her praises. She brought her to our room and they were up talking while I was in bed. I thought she seemed really lovely.

> 'THAT GIRL LOOKS SICK, SO COOL.'

JADE : I got on the bus to Boot Camp and the first person I met was Jesy. We sat next to each other and I looked at her and thought she was the coolest person ever with her huge curly blonde hair, massive glasses, colourful trainers and shorts. She was wacky and crazy and amazing – everything

up and, I don't know why, we started picking the bags up and swinging them round our heads. It was crazy, we were naughty.

JESY ⁑ We'd leave the rubbish in the corridor and forget to take it down and eventually it started smelling, which was awful. We'd had so many parties as well and I think maybe the music was too loud. We were just young girls having fun and the landlord wasn't very happy, so in the end we had to get out, but it was fine. We were both in relationships and wanted our own space, and it was costing so much money to live there. In the beginning you don't care, then you start to think there's no point throwing money down the drain when you want to save up for a house. I did rent a place on my own for a while but didn't like living by myself. I found it scary not having someone else around so I moved back home.

LEIGH-ANNE ⁑ We kept having problems with things in the flat, like the air conditioning, but when the guy would come out to look at it there'd be nothing wrong, it was just that we didn't know how to work it. One time the dishwasher went funny and we called someone out and it turned out it was working fine. I think the landlord got fed up. He messaged us, and the tone was quite rude so Jesy replied and gave him a piece of her mind. Oh god! After six months, when our lease came up for renewal, he evicted us. We loved the flat and didn't want to go at all. We were practically begging to stay but he was having none of it.

WE'D HAD SO MANY PARTIES...AND I THINK MAYBE THE MUSIC WAS TOO LOUD. WE WERE JUST YOUNG GIRLS HAVING FUN.

I got a flat on my own on Oxford Gardens, in Ladbroke Grove, and it was lovely, but if my boyfriend wasn't staying over I'd get scared. I hated being on my own. Some nights I wouldn't sleep. I'd think I could hear stuff or that there was someone on the balcony outside my bedroom coming to get me. Ladbroke Grove was one of those places where you'd walk round and it was lovely, then all of a sudden you'd be in a bit of a rough area, which was quite scary. I wanted to save up to buy somewhere as well so before very long, about a year after winning *The X Factor*, I moved back home.

'We're gonna stick together,
know we'll get through it all'
'CHANGE YOUR LIFE'

PERRIE: In the first year of Little Mix we were ill all the time. Me and Jade have awful immune systems. If I get ill, she catches it, and if she's ill, I get the same thing. Trying to juggle your life is really hard, even getting an appointment with the doctor or dentist is a battle, because you never have time for anything.

I constantly had tonsillitis but thought I was just stressed and run down from working hard. I kept getting ill, and because we were so busy there was no time to recover properly and my tonsils were getting worse and worse. I was taking antibiotics but you can't keep doing that because after a while they stop working. It got so my tonsils hurt all the time. I'd wake up every morning in agony, not able to breathe properly. The more I worked, the more I sang, and the bigger my tonsils got. This went on for about a year and it got to the point where I was finding it hard to sing. I'd take paracetamol for the pain, feel OK for a few hours and just keep going. I think in the beginning you're always scared of doing something wrong and you don't want to upset anyone or let anyone down so you carry on. The adrenalin helps. Now, when I think back, I don't know how I did it.

Eventually, I went to see a specialist and by then my tonsils were *huge*. He was shocked, baffled I'd managed to keep going so long and didn't understand how I could talk, never mind sing. He asked about my breathing and if I was able to sleep. I was in so much pain I wasn't sleeping well at all and I snored so badly I used to wake myself up. When me and Jade lived in the Notting Hill flat she could hear me snoring through the wall, which was horrendous.

I was told I had to have my tonsils taken out and I was terrified, thinking my voice would change or I wouldn't be able to sing any more. I was really worried I'd lose my job. I went to see a few specialists and took Meg, my vocal coach, with me. Everyone was 100 per cent certain I'd be fine and that, if anything, my voice would be stronger and I'd be able to sing louder and higher than ever, so I agreed to the op. I couldn't have carried on the way I was anyway. I was still panicking though, frightened they'd hit my vocal chords, but everyone was confident it would be fine.

The girls had to do a few shows without me, in December 2012, while I recovered. I was on a lot of medication, out of it, sleeping most of the time, and it took a good month before I was better. I really missed the girls. I'd see them performing on TV and feel left out. I was desperate to get back on stage with them.

The first night I was home after I came out of hospital Mam was looking after me, and she panicked because when I went to sleep I was completely silent. She was so used to me snoring like an old man she started shaking me, calling my name, to make sure I was still breathing.

To start with all I could eat was ice cream and mash, stuff like that, and I was in a lot of pain. I'd been told to rest my voice but I was desperate to know if I could still sing. After three days I tried singing and when nothing came out I broke down, crying. My mam knew it was way too soon and told me I needed to rest and do as I was told!

It sounds gross but after the surgery you have scabs on the back of your throat and they have to come off, so I was told to eat toast and crisps and dry food because that helps you heal but it hurt eating stuff like that. Anything with salt in it would burn and sting. As my throat got better I started doing the exercises my vocal coach had given me and they really helped strengthen everything. Our first tour, *DNA*, was to start in January 2013, so I knew I had to be fit and ready for that – and I was.

My voice changed completely. Straight after the operation it was a lot higher. I feel it's back to normal now, huskier again. Having surgery was the best thing because, touch wood, I've not had any problems since.

> I REALLY MISSED THE GIRLS. I'D SEE THEM PERFORMING ON TV AND FEEL LEFT OUT. I WAS DESPERATE TO GET BACK ON STAGE WITH THEM.

JESY ⁑ Being in a group, I naturally stood out because the other girls were a lot slimmer than me, a lot smaller, and I got a lot of bullying on social media about my weight. In

the *X Factor* house, stuck indoors, not allowed out, not getting any exercise, I got into bad eating habits and put on weight, but it all came off naturally afterwards. I'd had bullying at school but people saying nasty things about me so publicly was a shock. I'd never experienced anything like it and didn't know what I'd done to make them be so horrible. You can read a hundred nice comments about yourself but it's the one nasty remark that plays over and over in your head. It can tear you apart. I really took it to heart, became obsessed with it, and that's not healthy.

Much as I wanted to be a singer, I felt I'd been happier before as a barmaid. I never expected all the rubbish that came from winning the show, and being in the band.

Nothing can prepare you for online abuse. I hate that it happened, because I could have enjoyed it all so much more if I hadn't become obsessed by the horrible stuff people were saying.

I remember in the beginning, when we'd just come off *The X Factor*, on the day of a photo shoot someone sent me a message on Facebook saying I was fat, the ugliest person in the world, and they wanted me to die. I cried and cried. I felt so uncomfortable having pictures taken and trying to feel good about myself, and at the same time I felt bad for the girls, because they were so excited and happy, and it was fun for them, but I could not think of anything worse to do that day. It was awful. When I look back on those early pictures I can see how sad I look compared to now, when I'm happy, and it's such a shame. I let it affect me so much that it took away a big part of my enjoyment of the whole experience and I'll never get that back.

I'D HAD BULLYING AT SCHOOL BUT PEOPLE SAYING NASTY THINGS ABOUT ME SO PUBLICLY WAS A SHOCK.

The girls were massively important. We'd do anything for each other and they were supportive, but at the same time I don't think they knew how bad things were because I used to hold it in as much as I could. I didn't tell anyone, not even them, how I really felt; then I'd go home and my pillow would get the brunt of the tears.

Nothing can prepare you for all the rubbish and abuse. It's horrific. I think what made it worse was that the other girls were getting such lovely comments, and I was thinking, 'What am I doing wrong? I don't understand.' I thought everyone hated me and got so obsessed about stupid comments from online trolls. I still don't understand how people can attack someone like that, when they don't even know them. I think you must have to have a really cold heart to be so vicious.

NOTHING CAN PREPARE YOU FOR ALL THE RUBBISH AND ABUSE. IT'S HORRIFIC.

It got to the point where even the fans noticed I was down and would ask if I was all right, saying I seemed really sad. In this business you have to come across as being happy for everyone, no matter how you feel, and it's not always easy.

I was so sad, but I was also thinking, 'I'm not this person, I'm a happy, bubbly person. I can't keep waking up feeling like this every day or I'll look back and regret it.' Now I'm older and I've been in the industry a bit longer I know it happens to everyone – that even the most beautiful girls, the skinniest girls, get stick. I met Nicola Roberts from Girls Aloud and she said, 'Why are you reading it? It's the worst thing you can do. If you stop, you'll feel much better.' So I took her advice and gradually trained myself not to look at social media.

I feel completely different about myself now. I never used to leave the house without being made up with my lashes on, but now I'm always going out bare-faced. I feel confident and beautiful without make-up.

When I think back I don't know how I lived my life reading all the rubbish about me and getting so down about it. I've learned that you can avoid negative crap by refusing to acknowledge it and by only entertaining positive energy in your life. As I always say, 'Never try to be anyone else other than you – you are beautiful and if we all looked the same, the world would be boring!'

JADE ✲ I feel very protective of Jesy. What happened to her was horrible. I still can't get over how people can be so nasty to someone they haven't ever met. Maybe they think we don't have feelings. It's horrible to see your best friend have her confidence chipped away by every comment and story that appears. I've had to learn not to answer back because the more you say the more it draws attention to it and makes things worse, so you have to ignore it and learn to grow a thick skin. Perrie's received a lot of hate stuff as well and all you can do is be there for them. We go through stuff and no one else knows what it feels like. I think that's why we have such a special friendship and are so close.

LEIGH-ANNE ✲ All of us have our insecurities and stuff we're dealing with and we're there for each other 100 per cent. We're best friends, we get on and have so much fun.

In the beginning we were thrown into a life of early starts, late nights, not a lot of sleep. You don't get a minute to breathe. We were suddenly famous and I don't think any of us were prepared for what that meant. It's hard to explain but it's almost like you're not a person any more. You're no longer Leigh-Anne from High Wycombe, you're this object – a pop star – and you have to learn to deal with it, which is very strange because of course we're really just normal human beings. Once you become public property people will shout at you in the street: 'There's that girl from Little Mix!'

Sometimes you're out, no make-up on, just going about your day, and people will come up wanting a picture and it might be the last thing you want but you can't turn them down. I'm conscious that first impressions are everything so, however I'm feeling, I don't say no to people. To be honest, I do sometimes think it would be nice if there was a cut-off point where you could be yourself and not have to think about being approached but at the same time our fans are incredible and we appreciate everything we have.

> **WE WERE SUDDENLY FAMOUS AND I DON'T THINK ANY OF US WERE PREPARED FOR WHAT THAT MEANT.**

When I first went on *The X Factor* I discovered that being on TV every week means people go on social media to say exactly what they think of you. I had no problem with my voice, my ability – I always believed in myself that way – but on the show I got quite a bit of stick from people saying my voice wasn't as strong as the rest of the girls. I didn't expect that kind of criticism and it affected me. I'm in a group with three girls who have incredible voices but at the same time I love my own voice and I've worked so hard and pushed myself to the point where I'm singing notes I wouldn't ever have thought possible. When I saw some of the comments I started to question myself. It's horrific how the negative stuff can get under your skin and affect you. It's easy to let every little thing bother you because there's so much pressure. You start questioning, 'Am I good enough? Do I deserve to be in this band?' So frustrating. What I love about the four of us is

we're so strong as friends. I couldn't ask to be in a group with three more amazing girls. They're so understanding and caring. There's no one going, 'Oh, I'm the leader.'

I don't know how solo artists do it. I need to go through the experience with people I know I can talk to and relate to. Without that I don't know what I would do.

I still get people now saying I'm not as strong a singer as the others and it's become an added pressure for me. Having that in the back of my head makes it ten times harder to perform on stage. I'll be coming up to the point where it's me singing my bit, thinking, 'Am I going to be OK?' I need to let that go because I know it's destructive and could end up ruining a lot of things. I do still believe in myself. I think you have to. If you don't, no one else will. That's why I've got 'Believe' tattooed on my neck.

I really feel I'm so lucky to be where I am, having an amazing time with three incredible girls. I'm a damn sight happier than I have ever been in my life. I've made my dream come true. How many people can say that?

PERRIE: If any of us get stick, we rally round each other. In the beginning we were very young, and *The X Factor* is a massive platform so everyone had a chance to comment on our hair and make-up, what we wore, what we looked like. I didn't know every little thing would be scrutinized – that was a shock and quite scary. When I saw some of the cruel comments online I thought, 'Why would they say that? Why would anyone want to bring someone down and make them feel bad?' I really could not get my head round it. It was horrible for Jesy.

A few years ago if I saw something horrible about me I cried. Now I know you've got to ignore it. Social media is like being in the playground but on a bigger, more

| A LITTLE DREAM, A LOT OF LOVE

messed-up scale. If you're confident in yourself, you'll be fine. These people making nasty comments don't know us. I know everyone has an opinion and I'm cool with that, but not when it's cruel.

JADE ⁑ I think people can relate to us and aspire to what we're doing because we're just ourselves – four normal girls who've had their ups and downs in life and wanted to sing and be something, and were lucky enough to have got there. It doesn't usually happen to people like us.

It's hard to adjust to getting recognized and being scrutinized and stories and pictures appearing in the press. When I lived in Notting Hill I didn't know the paparazzi knew my address so I'd come out of the house and get photographed looking absolutely rotten! The next day in the paper the headline would be: 'JADE WITH NO MAKE-UP ON!' I'd be thinking, 'Leave me alone. I'm a young girl. Sorry if I've got spots – what do you want me to do?'

It's weird as well going out and people wanting your picture. Even now sometimes I react a bit awkwardly to it because I don't quite know what to say or how to deal with it. At the same time it's incredible that we have fans who love us. I think our fan base is really lovely.

When we started out the majority were young girls, who have grown up with us, and we had this image of making sure girls were nice to other girls and being confident within themselves.

We sat down and thought about the kind of sound we were going for, the image we wanted, and felt there was a gap for a girl band that was very much girls for girls and not too sexualized or intimidating. We wanted to fill that gap and write the kind of music we would want to listen to, to make us feel better. That's how it all came about.

PERRIE: We all look out for each other. I still have a problem with my oesophagus from when I was little and every now and then my food gets stuck and I can't get it down. I never know when it's going to happen and if I'm in meetings or out for a meal or something I have to get up and run to the toilet. The girls know what's going on if I suddenly go quiet and they'll take me out. They've always got my back.

In the summer of 2014 we were in America doing a radio show, about to do a meet and greet and perform for fans, and were in a restaurant where they'd done us lovely food. I suddenly realized mine was stuck. There was nothing I could do. I tried having a drink but it didn't help and when it got to ten minutes before we were due to go on I was starting to panic. Annecka, our manager, was getting desperate, coming out with mad stuff like, 'Have some fizzy Coke.' 'Try jumping up and down.' 'Try being sick.' So I was drinking Coke and jumping up and down and trying to be sick … and it made no difference. In the end, the girls had to perform without me. I felt awful but it's just one of those things. We're there for each other and if something goes wrong for one of us, the others step in. That's how it works.

JESY: I think we're so lucky to have each other. You never know what might have happened if it hadn't been the four of us together. It's weird because being in Little Mix I know for a fact my life has changed hugely and at the same time I don't feel any different. My family and friends think I'm exactly the same as I always was. I'd be gutted if they thought I'd changed. I would never want that. I can understand why some solo artists end up going a bit mental. Some people get really affected by the industry and being well known, and not in a nice way. We keep each other sane and grounded. The others are with me, every step of the way, and I feel very, very lucky to be in a group with my three best friends.

JADE ⁑ When I was little my mam was obsessed with Diana Ross and looked just like her. She had the big hair, gorgeous big brown eyes, and when she went to the bingo with my Great-Auntie Norma she used to say she was going to do a concert. She kept it going for ages and I was convinced she really was Diana Ross. That was who I wanted to be. I idolized her. At the school disco I'd turn up in a chiffon fishtail dress with my hair all brushed out thinking I was Diana Ross! All the other kids were into Vengaboys but I was listening to Diana Ross and the Supremes and learning Motown music, which was how I started singing, so really it was all down to my mam.

I was about ten when Mam told me she wasn't really Diana Ross . . . I was heartbroken! I couldn't believe she'd had me fooled all that time. By then I was sending tapes to TV's *Stars in Their Eyes*, trying to get on the show as Diana Ross. I was so determined. When they rang and said they wanted me on I was over the moon, but it was a family special and no one in my family would come on it with me. I was devastated.

Thanks to my mam, I'm still obsessed with Diana Ross. She's my icon.

My dad loves Michael Jackson and all the golden oldies, although he listens to a lot of current music on the radio in his car all day. When he's drunk he likes to sing a bit of Elvis on the karaoke, but I don't think I get my voice from him, ha ha. Karl would kill me for saying it, but he's a really good singer. I used to listen to him singing or MCing in his bedroom but as soon as I'd open the door he'd stop. Spoilsport! My cousin Zoe Badwi is a famous singer in Australia – she's amazing – but I think that's as far as it goes in my family in terms of musicality.

THANKS TO MY MAM, I'M STILL OBSESSED WITH DIANA ROSS. SHE'S MY ICON.

My mam tried to take me to stage school when I was little – I hated it and cried my eyes out. When everyone around you is confident and willing to get up and give what they've got it can make you feel even more insecure.

I remember going to Sunderland to audition for *West Side Story* when I was about fourteen and seeing everyone else being super-confident, singing at the top of their voices, and feeling sick with nerves. I knew I couldn't do it. I was a right little wimp, scared of my own shadow. My mam couldn't understand because at home I'd sing songs from *My Fair Lady*, getting right into character, so she thought I'd be perfect for musical theatre, but I was so shy. When I walked out of the Sunderland auditions I think it was just about the last straw for her. She was heartbroken. I remember going home in the car, saying, 'Mam, I love you and you've done so much for me but you need to stop pushing me because it's scaring me and I'm feeling pressured.' She said she was only pushing me because she knew I was talented and didn't want to see a gift go to waste.

I CAN SEE NOW SHE HAD FAITH IN ME WHEN I HAD NONE IN MYSELF.

Around then I started doing the working men's clubs in the North East with my mam. At first I felt ill going on stage, overwhelmed. I remember singing 'I'm Alive' and shaking, thinking I really had to get my act together and go for it. Everyone got up and started clapping and I was like, 'Oh my god, they liked it!' That gave me a hunger and I decided to practise a few more songs. Mam got another girl in, Carly McKeith, and we called ourselves The Sweethearts. We did all sorts – from Doris Day to songs from *Sister Act* and *Dreamgirls*. I started doing an Amy Winehouse tribute act – I had the wig, the leggings, everything – and got a good reaction, which gave me more confidence.

It got so I used to look forward to going to work in the clubs at the weekend. My friends had jobs in shops and were getting paid nearly nothing and I was getting £50 a night to sing, which was a fortune. This was all a year or two before I auditioned for *The X Factor* and without my mam taking me out to sing I don't know if I'd ever have given it a go. I went from zero confidence to believing I could maybe do it. Thanks, Mam!

JADE ✴ From when I was about twelve I wanted to be a singer. I did everything – amateur musicals at my local theatre, singing in pubs and old people's homes, a bit of 'Que Sera Sera' and Bette Midler. I sang in an Italian restaurant every week and I'd work Christmas Day and on my birthday, Boxing Day. My mam supported me and taxied me from place to place. She was always in the background with her little PA, helping me out.

I was about sixteen when I started doing working men's clubs and that's how I learned to talk to the audience and deal with being heckled, people telling me to get off! I remember once singing 'The Rose', by Bette Midler, and everyone thought I'd finished and started clapping and I was like, 'I've not finished yet.' Some man shouted, 'I fucking wish you had!' I just carried on because I didn't know what else to do. It was horrible but funny as well, and you learn how to deal with people like that and get over it.

In the restaurant where I sang they were always telling me to turn it down! A guy from a label came in one day and scouted me, wanting to sign me. He reeled off the names boots Nadia gave me to audition in. She was a beautiful, talented, kind woman. She was a performer and we'd done shows together. One show we did, *Rent*, has a song in it called 'No Day But Today', and it became a bit of a motto for our group of friends. When Nadia died it really affected me, and it made me realize you don't know how long you're going to be here so it's important to do what you want with your life.

The first time I auditioned for *The X Factor*, in 2008, when I got to Boot Camp and then no further, I was broken-hearted. It felt like the end of the world. Cheryl was a judge that year and came and spoke to me. She was like, 'You're just too young. Come back in a couple of years and you'll make it.' In 2010 I went back with Liam Payne, who I'd met at the auditions two years earlier, and got through to Boot Camp again and that was when I met the rest of the One Direction lads. They'd just got put in a group and I really thought I would get put in a girl group, so when I didn't I was absolutely devastated. Cher Lloyd was there that year and she was really fierce for her age. I think, personality-wise, she kind of overpowered me.

CHER LLOYD WAS THERE THAT YEAR AND SHE WAS REALLY FIERCE FOR HER AGE.

I wasn't going to audition in 2011. The thought of putting myself through it all again, and the embarrassment of having to come back to South Shields and tell everyone I didn't make it, was too much. My boyfriend didn't want me to have another go. Maybe he thought if I did well it would be the end of us, which was what happened eventually, although it was an amicable split.

It was my mam and brother who pushed me to have another go. Mam was like, 'Go on – what have you got to

lose? Third time lucky!' I was inspired as well by Nadia, and thought, 'Fine, I'll give it another go.' You've got to keep trying, haven't you? I still wasn't really expecting anything to happen but it paid off. Mam and Karl were right – I won!

LEIGH-ANNE ✻ In 2011 I think I was going through a bit of a crisis in my life, working part-time in Pizza Hut, writing my music, going back and forth to the studio, doing songs, nothing ever coming of it. One day I was just sitting around at home and thought I might as well have a go at *The X Factor*. What did I have to lose? My dad told me to get some girls together and perform as a group and I was like, 'No, I'm not doing that. I want to be a solo artist.'

LITTLE DID I KNOW.

Once I applied to *The X Factor* things took off. I auditioned at the O2, in London, and took my mum and dad, Sairah, and my friends Hannah and Rosie with me. I've still got the poster they made: 'Leigh-Anne's got the X Factor!' It was so important having their support. Those people in particular have been there from the start and have always believed in me, even before *The X Factor*, so it meant a lot to have them with me at the moment in my life when everything began to change. When I auditioned I had a whole new lease of confidence. I knew I was going to sing Rihanna's 'Only Girl (in the World)' and when I got on stage I don't know what happened, it was like I was watching the whole thing on TV. I went from being the shy girl in the corner at stage school to really going for it, jumping up and down, giving it my all. Sairah couldn't believe the change in me; she said, 'Where

did that come from?' I really don't know. It came out of nowhere. I'd never been like that before. The experience did something to me. I felt I was supposed to be there, as if it was fate; that it was all planned out for me.

PERRIE: Even though I'd been doing the clubs and enjoyed getting a reaction, I still wasn't confident when it came to performing on my own. After school I'd gone to Newcastle College to study performing arts, thinking I'd be a drama teacher. I was still scared of auditioning but all those times when my mam tried to push me and I'd dug my heels in must have made an impact because they were putting on a variety show at college and I decided to audition. I would only have to sing in front of my form tutor, Steve Halliday, and I knew he wouldn't judge me harshly. I got every part I went for! Mam was like, 'Does that not tell you something?'

It was my mam who applied to *The X Factor* for me. I remember trying to get out of it, thinking people would laugh at me, and Mam saying I'd win. I was like, 'Mam, you're biased.'

I was supposed to audition in Newcastle but the night before it was announced on the internet that it had been cancelled. I was so thankful! At four in the morning Mam came into my room with a bit of breakfast and told me to get up and get ready, we were going to Glasgow to audition there. I thought, 'No, this is not happening.' Mam packed a bag and dragged me to the car. I kept saying I didn't want to go and she said, 'I've done everything I could in my life for you, so please do this one thing for me.'

I WAS SUPPOSED TO AUDITION IN NEWCASTLE BUT THE NIGHT BEFORE IT WAS ANNOUNCED ON THE INTERNET THAT IT HAD BEEN CANCELLED. I WAS SO THANKFUL!

SHE GUILT-TRIPPED ME, BASICALLY!

I was convinced I'd get a 'no' and be humiliated. At the audition I sang Beyoncé's 'Ave Maria' and Alanis Morissette's 'You Oughta Know', and I was shaking so much my voice sounded like Larry the Lamb. I'd been nervous before but never like that. I couldn't believe it when I got through to the next round. I thought I'd get to see the judges then but there were about three more stages first.

At the next audition my dad came as well, and my brother and nana. I wore a hippy dress and had a little gold bag and had to go into a room and sing in front of a couple more production people. Every time I started singing one of them would put up a hand and stop me. She was like, 'Have you got anything else?' I sang seven or eight songs and she stopped me every time before I got to the good part. I was getting frustrated and in the end I started crying and said, 'I'm not going to get through if you keep stopping me.' She said I was already through, they just wanted to hear what I could do.

I had to wait all day to see the judges and every time the camera came round I hid behind my hair. but I couldn't avoid them forever. They wanted to know about my dress and my style and before I knew it I was being interviewed. I caught my dad's eye and he was winking, trying to make me smile, and I thought, 'This is mad.' Afterwards Dad said, 'You've done all the hard work – now go and do what you were born to do, and sing.'

I remember walking on stage at the SECC in Glasgow and thinking it was massive, a lot different to how it looked on TV. I sang 'You Oughta Know' and Tulisa stopped me. She thought it was too old for me. I did 'Ave Maria' a cappella and Tulisa and Louis Walsh didn't like it but Gary Barlow

LEIGH-ANNE ⁂ It's overwhelming for my family seeing their little girl make her dream come true. I'm doing what I always wanted to do, singing and performing – selling out the O2 Arena, which we did for the first time on the *Salute* tour, in 2014, is incredible. I'm *very* lucky, and they're so proud. At the same time, I don't feel famous; I don't think any of us do. The success we've had hasn't gone to our heads and the people who know us say we haven't changed a bit. We don't have a team of people running round doing everything for us. I still do normal things same as I used to, like shop for pyjamas and fluffy socks at Primark. I don't get it when pop stars are horrible to everyone. Why? They're no better than anyone else.

I do miss out on stuff at home, with being away a lot, and I can't always see my family and friends when I want to, which is sometimes difficult. My little nephew Kailum goes to Barbara Speake's Stage School and he's such a little star, wants to be in the limelight all the time. I was gutted when I missed one of his shows. When I got to see my niece's nativity show and saw how cute Faith was on stage I was so happy. I missed my best friend Hannah's graduation, and she was upset about it. I hated that I couldn't be there but, hard as it is, it comes with the job. I'm lucky because I know my relationships are strong enough to survive me being away so much of the time. I can't really put into words how important my family is. If I didn't have them, I wouldn't be able to do this job. I need the stability, the normality they give me. Although they're crazy, I love them for it!

JADE ⁂ I think my family is a bit overwhelmed by everything that's happened to me. My brother doesn't get soppy often but when we did the Brits, in February 2016, he sent me a text saying how proud he was and how much he loves me. I think my dad and I make more of an effort with each other than we did before, because we know time is precious. I do miss out on stuff at home because I'm away a lot, and sometimes I feel guilty. My nephew is four and every time I see him he's changed. It's like he went from being a baby to a toddler and I missed all the stages in between, but I'm the cool auntie so that's OK. My niece Leoni is turning into a beautiful young woman and it bloody scares me every time I come home! Karl and his fiancée, Shireen, have had a gorgeous little girl and I missed the whole pregnancy. A couple of years back my best friend, Holly, had a boyfriend I never got to meet, then they split up and I wasn't there to support her. I didn't even know what had gone on. Anna's dad passed away and I feel like I wasn't there enough to support her. Things like that I feel bad about, so I try to ring or message everyone at least once a week. You can't take anyone for granted.

We were rehearsing the *X Factor* tour and recording our first album, *DNA*, in 2012, when my mam had a stroke. I got a call saying I had to come home. I'm always worrying about my mam anyway, with her lupus, so I knew something wasn't right, and when I got back and my mam wasn't at home I had the worst feeling. My Great-Auntie Norma was there and told me Mam was in hospital. That night she had two more strokes. It was so tough seeing her ill. At times like that you feel guilty that you can't be with your family all the time. I just wanted to look after her.

I stayed in the North East until I was sure she was all right. I'm always a bit on edge about her now, but she made a good recovery. She can't write well any more and her memory isn't what it used to be. But she's in a really good place at the minute, content. She's independent, out with friends all the time and enjoying being a nanna. It's the

JADE ⁑ Up until about a year and a half ago I absolutely hated living in London, just because it was too big for me. When I was in Notting Hill I didn't like coming out of the house and not knowing anyone, not having a sense of where I was. I did have a boyfriend, Sam, and I quite liked east London when we moved there, but when we split up, in 2015, and I was in the flat by myself and so lonely I didn't really know what to do.

I'd met Sam through Jesy when I came off *The X Factor*. He was in Diversity and she was seeing someone in the group as well, so that's how we got together. It moved fast for how young I was but we had a good relationship, a good time. I think as we got older we realized we were a bit too different. We did try for a long time to make it work but couldn't and, in the end, we were better off as friends. He was a good supportive person to be around and he was there a lot during the time I was feeling down and lonely in London, so it's a chapter of my life I don't regret at all. I'll always support him and the lads. Obviously, no break-up is nice but it didn't end sourly.

After we split up I was in the flat by myself a lot, too scared to go out because I didn't know many people. I'd been so used to having people around me in South Shields, everyone five minutes away at the most. I'd ring my mam, upset, and say I wanted to come home and she'd say, 'Go on, pet, you'll be fine,' and she'd come down and look after me and cook for me. My friends would come down and make me feel better. I was feeling a bit sorry for myself, thinking, 'I hate London, nobody's nice here, nobody says hello to me in the street.' I found it really hard, so different to what I was used to in South Shields.

It wasn't until I forced myself to go out and make friends that I started to like London. It's not easy but people from the

When I'm away from work I'm open to any kind of music: R&B, hip hop, Missy Elliott, Beyoncé. I love Beyoncé's 'Smash Into You' because when me and the girls got together we used to play it all the time and it brings back lots of memories. 'Run the World (Girls)' by Beyoncé is another favourite – it's our go-to song when we're getting geared up to go on stage. I used to listen to Justin Timberlake a lot when I was younger, stuff like 'Like I Love You'. I still love the Spice Girls – 'Viva Forever' and 'Spice Up Your Life'. I love a girly sleepover; for my twenty-fourth birthday, in 2015, I went round to Perrie's with the other girls to celebrate. We went to the supermarket and bought an unnecessary amount of food – piled up a trolley with chocolate and sweets, nachos, birthday cake – got into our 'Black Magic' onesies and watched the *Spice World* movie. Perrie had a massive bed at the time and we all slept in that.

LEIGH-ANNE : I can spend a long time getting ready to go out, hours. I have no sense of time-keeping and my best friend, Hannah, is the same. We spend so much time faffing we're always late. I've always been the party girl in the group. I love clubbing but the clubs I really liked in London, Amika and Anaya, have shut down. I think some London clubs are so pretentious and the men at the door can be so rude. I despise that. After bad experiences at a couple of clubs, Libertine and DSTRKT, I'll never go back.

When I'm out I love a good cocktail, anything fruity. I like rum punch, champagne, Prosecco. Vodka and tonic is my go-to drink. My favourite places to eat in London are Nobu, Hakkasan and Muse of Mayfair.

I love going home and chilling out, having a night in. I'll get a takeaway, Indian or a pizza, and put on a good film. I love watching series like *Game of Thrones*. There's an you go to touch her, she'll cringe and go the opposite way. I've got a Pomeranian called Hachi, after the film *Hachi: A Dog's Tale*. He's a reddish gingery colour with a thick mane, like a little lion, and he is my baby. I got him as a puppy and he's three now. I've trained him to sit, give a paw, duck and roll over. He's so funny. If he's done something wrong, his Elvis lip twitches until I tell him it's OK, he's not in trouble, then he smiles. If I'm crying, he cries, jumps up and licks my tears. He is my best friend. I've got a little teacup Yorkie, Teddy, as well. She is gorgeous, so tiny, a real little madam. When I take her for a walk the biggest dog can come over and she'll give it what-for.

I've got a cinema room with an L-shaped leather sofa and I love being in there, in jogging bottoms and a hoody, thick cosy socks, relaxing with a glass of wine. On TV I love *Catchphrase* – shouting the answers at the telly! – *TOWIE*, *Geordie Shore*, *Ant and Dec's Saturday Night Takeaway*. I'll watch anything to do with property: *Grand Designs*, *A Place in the Sun*, *Homes under the Hammer*.

IF I'M CRYING, HE CRIES, JUMPS UP AND LICKS MY TEARS. HE IS MY BEST FRIEND.

If I'm having a night in, I love a takeaway and alternate between Chinese and Indian. Curry is my favourite. If I've got friends round, I'll order the world so we can pick. If it's just me, it'll be chicken tikka masala, pilau rice and Peshwari naan, which is quite sweet. I love kulfi but my favourite dessert is rasmalai. It's a kind of dumpling in a really sweet creamy milk and you eat it cold. The texture and flavour are definitely not to everyone's taste – when my cousin, Ellie, tried it she spat it out and said it was like sweet scrambled egg. I absolutely love it. Just talking about it makes me crave it. I learned how to make it but when I saw the amount of cream and sugar that went into it I thought, 'OK, maybe I won't be eating it every night . . .'

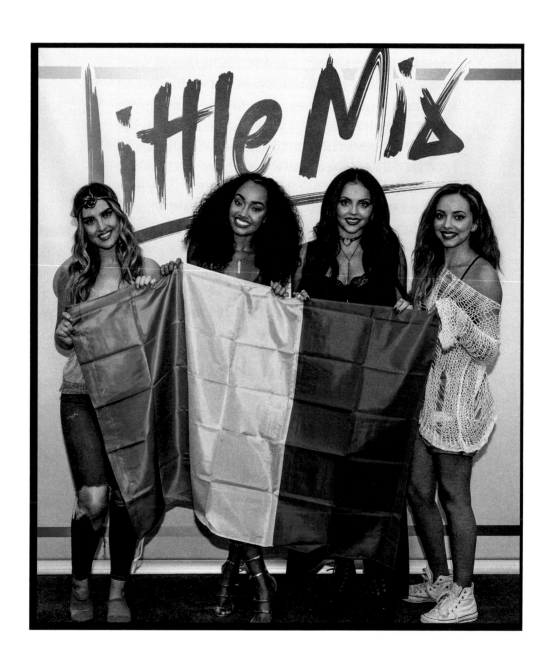

PERRIE: I absolutely love travelling and Japan is my favourite place in the world. I love the people, the culture, the shopping – the Harajuku girls in their crazy clothes. It's a wacky, cool place, on a whole other level. There's one long street, Takeshita Street, in Tokyo, full of little pancake stalls, vintage shops and quirky places where you can get mad things like prams for dogs. It's a different world, like being in a colourful animated film. People from our Japanese label came to see our first tour, *DNA*, in 2013, and we knew we had to impress them. They loved the show and flew us out not long after. I wasn't sure what to expect – I was picturing escalators, people on hover boards in the middle of the street, but there are lots of beautiful old temples as well as the high-rise buildings and wacky stuff.

That first trip, I wasn't all that keen on the food. Fish and lobsters in tanks looking at you before you eat them makes me feel funny, but I love *teppanyaki*, where they cook the food in front of you, and Kobe beef, rice and noodles. I find the country so fascinating I don't miss home at all. The only time I found it hard being away was when we were in America for two months straight, in 2014, on the Demi Lovato tour, and it felt like forever. We did three weeks of promos, then the tour and were constantly on the go, and I felt really homesick. I absolutely loved performing but as soon as we'd come off stage I wanted to go home. I had a boyfriend then and kept to myself and wasn't happy. I was on the phone home the whole time. My bill was horrendous.

I've got a different thought process about everything now and I'm excited to enjoy my life and be on the road touring. It might not last forever so you've got to make

JAPAN IS MY FAVOURITE PLACE IN THE WORLD. I LOVE THE PEOPLE, THE CULTURE, THE SHOPPING.

pictures.' People probably thought I'd posed for them when I hadn't even known they were being taken. I cried my eyes out for weeks. The press know what they're doing. They'll find the most hideous picture of you and write a lovely comment – 'Jesy looking fabulous!' – knowing you'll get trolled. It makes me wonder how they can sleep at night.

Me and Jake have never been abroad on holiday and if we do, it will have to be to a private villa with a pool.

PERRIE⁘ I went to the Maldives at the beginning of 2016 and it was my best holiday ever. I really felt like I needed a break after a shitty year and wanted to begin the New Year as I meant to go on, make a fresh start. I'd never really gone wild and splashed out on a holiday so I decided to treat myself and took my mam, Aunty Nancy, my cousin, Ellie, and my sister, Caitlin. I wanted somewhere with good food, sunshine – where you could step straight out of your villa on to a beach with clear blue sea. I was at the travel agent looking at various places and nothing felt right until I saw a picture of the Maldives and straight away thought it looked like paradise, exactly what I was after.

Even the journey there was amazing. We landed at the airport and were whisked off on a tiny plane to another island. I was thinking, 'What now?' as we got into a speedboat for the last bit of the journey. When I saw our island appearing out of nowhere in the distance it was so beautiful I could have cried with happiness. We had a villa with a pool and the beach was right in front of us. White sand, hammocks – everywhere you looked was picturesque. It was so peaceful and relaxing, hardly anyone around, and I could really let my hair down.

I CRIED MY EYES OUT FOR WEEKS. THE PRESS KNOW WHAT THEY'RE DOING. THEY'LL FIND THE MOST HIDEOUS PICTURE OF YOU.

I FELT FREE AS A BIRD.

People think of the Maldives as a romantic couples'
retreat but it was great for a girly holiday. One day we took
a boat trip to a private island, had a picnic and went snorkelling.
There was so much to do: yoga, scuba diving, jet skiing,
dolphin cruises. We had bikes for getting round the island
so we cycled everywhere. On our way back to the villa one
night I was a bit tipsy. My phone was in the basket on the
front of my bike and I saw it flash. I made a grab for it and
next thing I went flying off the bike and into a tree. Everyone
was crying with laughter. I was laughing as well, going,
'Guys, I know it's funny but I think I've really hurt myself . . .'
When we got back to the villa and I took my dress off my
back and legs were scratched to shreds. I'd cut my head as
well, but not badly. It wasn't even anything important on
my phone, an Instagram alert or something, definitely
not worth crashing for.

What I'd love to do in future if we get a break is go to
America, hire a VW hippy van and do a big road trip. Drive
from LA through the desert to Vegas, do the whole Route 66
thing. Only trouble is I haven't passed my driving test! I've
had lessons and I can drive but I failed my theory test by one
point just before I did *The X Factor*, then I didn't get another
chance to take it until 2015. I failed again by a single point,
which made me think, 'Is that a sign? Am I not meant to be
driving?' I believe in stuff like that. If it's meant to be, it will
happen, at the right time, or maybe by the time I get a
chance to do the American road trip I'll have a boyfriend
who can drive.

Little Me

LEIGH-ANNE ✳ I've always been into fashion
and clothes and when I was younger I definitely used to
follow the trends. I remember wearing combat trousers
with tassels and those hideous medallion belts everyone
wore. So many things I look back on and think, 'So bad!'
When I was younger, going up to London to shop was a
special treat. I'd be given £50 to spend, which was a fortune,
get the train with my best friend and have a lovely day out.
You'd find me at Primark a lot, trying to make my money
go a bit further. River Island and Topshop were more
expensive but I loved them.

I have enjoyed exploring fashion over the years and love
discovering new brands. I have developed expensive taste
which is a bit of a problem lol but it's mainly because my
boyfriend at the time spoiled me and I guess you could say
he opened my eyes to some new brands and designers.
My style now is more my own though and will keep
evolving over time.

It's a way of defining myself. I wear what I want but I'd
describe my style as high fashion and I love experimenting
with new designers. Jane Bowler is amazing, and I love
Acne. A while ago I came across Marques' Almeida in
Harvey Nichols, in London. The clothes are cool, so
different. I bought two really unusual denim pieces that
go together, a top and a pair of jeans. I've since realized they
are quite the designers and Rihanna and Justin Bieber wear
their stuff. Fashion is there to be experimented with. I don't
think it's worth it if you don't take a risk so I will wear
anything. I love bright, vibrant colours – I think that's my
island side. Green is my favourite. White is good because it
brings out your tan. I wear a mix of high-end designers and
high street. I love Marques' Almeida, Acne, Dior, Chanel –
they're just some of my favourite designers but I love the

high street too. I think accessories are key. It's good to splash out on them because they're timeless and you'll have them forever, although I'm bad with sunglasses. I love Chanel and Dior but I've lost so many pairs. I have a thing for Louis Vuitton. Goya is an incredible luxury brand. I've got a lovely bag of theirs that my ex boyfriend bought for me. My biggest splurge was probably my Celine bag, I wear it all the time, though, so I don't feel bad. I appreciate everything I have because when I was fifteen, going to London with £50 to spend, I never ever thought I'd one day be able to buy Louis Vuitton or Celine. I don't take anything for granted.

I LOVE BRIGHT, VIBRANT COLOURS – I THINK THAT'S MY ISLAND SIDE. GREEN IS MY FAVOURITE.

I've got a lot of clothes and they take over the whole house. Every six weeks I have a clear-out and a tidy, but I can't keep up and within days it's messy again. I used to hoard things but now I make a conscious effort to get rid of stuff and give away whatever I don't wear any more. I have quite a few pairs of shoes. I remember my first pair of designer shoes, the Louboutins I got from management for my twenty-first birthday. They were classic black patent peep-toes, really high, with the red soles, and I was obsessed, strutting round in them. I've worn them so much they're pretty battered now. I also love Guiseppe Zanotti, but they're statement shoes for special occasions, so I don't wear them that much.

PERRIE: I like to mix it up, be fun and quirky. Growing up, if I saw someone wearing the same thing, I'd want to be different. I've got really cool parents. Dad's in a rock band so I love the ripped tee-shirts and jeans look, and denim, and Mam's an eighties chick. I'd ask what she used to wear when she was younger and do something similar – ripped jeans, a baggy denim jacket and a big belt. I'd go to college every day with a different look.

I think my style has evolved a lot. I don't follow trends, I wear what I like, the wackier the better. I'm a lot more body-confident now and I think that's a good thing. At one time I would never wear anything the slightest bit revealing. I wouldn't feel comfortable and didn't want to be thought slutty. I'd be going out in black every night, and my mam would be like, 'You're young, you've got a lovely figure. Why are you hiding it?'

I'm twenty-two now and I'm single so why not wear something I feel sexy in? Girls should encourage other girls to wear whatever makes them feel comfortable. If that means covering up, fine, but if you want to wear a skimpy outfit, that's OK as well. What I've learned is you don't dress to impress other people, you dress for yourself.

I've splurged a lot on shoes and bags. I've definitely got a weakness there. I love strappy heels, anything delicate. I don't like my whole foot covered. I've got some over-the-knee lace-up boots in a gorgeous nude shade that I wore to the 'Black Magic' number 1 party, in 2015. I've got them in black as well but I hardly ever wear them, they're such hard work to get on. My mam hates them because she has to lace them up for me. I've got hundreds of pairs of shoes and boots – my favourites are my strappy gladiator Versace boots. They're quite chunky with big pointy stiletto heels. I've got some Jimmy Choos, which are comfortable and not too high, good for dancing. If you've got a lot going on with your outfit, shoes should be minimal. and if your clothes are quite plain, go for crazy shoes.

I like to buy vintage because they're one-offs, and I also like Topshop, ASOS and Missguided. Urban Outfitters is another favourite. Growing up, I could never afford

All Saints and now I'll wear it head to toe. I love their jeans and leather jackets, holey tee-shirts. For socks and pyjamas I still shop at Primark.

In Japan I went a bit wild. Someone from our label there took me to a cool little vintage shop down a back alley off Takeshita Street that sold original tour tees – everything from Bon Jovi to Guns N' Roses – and I spent about £800 on three tee-shirts.

JADE ⁂ Growing up I copied what everyone else was wearing and tried to fit in, then when I got a bit older I wanted to stand out a little and I experimented with styles and wacky colours, but it's hard in a small town to dress a bit more wild. When we became Little Mix it was a case of anything goes, and I feel like the girls have helped me express myself more with fashion. I'd say my style is a bit boyish – I like tailoring and suits and I've always liked wearing shirts, bow ties and braces. I like brands like The Kooples that get the whole boy-style that's good for girls, and if I could afford it, I'd wear Vivienne Westwood and Alexander McQueen. When we're on the road I don't have time to put a good outfit together. I'm writing this on tour, at the venue in Brighton, a few hours before we go on, and I've just realized I'm in my Christmas socks, butterfly leggings and a Princess Jasmine jumper... not the most stylish outfit I've ever worn!

I love shoes and I've got hundreds of pairs, but I never wear them; they just look lovely on the shelf. One of my first splurges was a pair of designer shoes just after I'd won *The X Factor*. I'd paid for me and my mam and two best friends to go on holiday. I was like, 'Where do all the pop stars go? Oh, everyone goes to Marbella when they've made it.' So that's where we went and I hated it, it was so pretentious. We went into a designer store and I think we had an Asda carrier bag

that we'd put our towels in and the woman in the shop gave us the snottiest look ever. It was obvious she thought we couldn't afford anything so we might as well leave. I think because she had that attitude I picked up the most expensive pair of shoes and said I'd have them. They were beautiful: Philipp Plein, black, really high, with Swarovski crystals on the heels. Mam was like, 'Go on, pet, you've earned it.' They cost about 3,000 euros and as soon as I walked out of the shop I thought, 'What have I done?' When I think about it now I feel sick, but I'd never been in that position before, wanting to prove a point because someone was looking down on me so much. I think I only wore them once, in America, and they were so painful I never put them on again, so that was my lesson in not buying ridiculous expensive things.

I LOVE SHOES AND I'VE GOT HUNDREDS OF PAIRS, BUT I NEVER WEAR THEM; THEY JUST LOOK LOVELY ON THE SHELF.

When I broke up with my boyfriend Sam I had a little splurge on the internet, crying into my ice cream, buying things to make me feel better. Anything Disney and I'm sold, so I got a Givenchy bag with Bambi on it and kept buying the whole collection until I knew I'd spent too much. I do use them, though. I'm not a big spender now and rarely buy things for myself.

JESY: When I was younger I was a dancer and constantly in baggy trousers and tops, always wanting to be comfy. I never showed off my figure. When I auditioned for *The X Factor* it wasn't that I was eccentric in how I dressed but I wore very bright stuff, and weird and wonderful Mickey Mouse trainers that were definitely a talking point and got me noticed. Everyone was saying, 'Oh my god, your trainers are amazing,' and I thought, 'I'm in here!'

On *The X Factor* they wanted me to try new things, like they put me in leggings, which were so out of my comfort zone, then after the show when I lost weight and got more confident I started trying out new styles. I was still in baggy tops but wearing leggings and heels, which I never would have done before. I think I experiment more now that I'm older, and when I look back at how I used to dress I think, '*Why* did I wear that?!'

Before Little Mix I was obsessed with trainers and when I had money from dancing I'd go up to London and buy a new pair. I loved the designer Jeremy Scott – the Mickey Mouse trainers I wore for my audition were his – and I got the last pair in the world, so I know they're worth a lot of money now. They're still my favourites. Altogether, I've got about 400 pairs, all boxed up, taking up loads of room. I don't know what to do with them. Some I've hardly worn, some still have their tags on. I've got some limited editions, some really expensive ones. I think the most I paid was about £900 for a pair with little encrusted crystals. I can't remember who the designer was and I never even wore them that much because I was scared of the crystals falling out. Now it seems ridiculous and I don't know why I paid all that money, but at the time I'd never seen anything like them and I had to have them. I don't ever wear trainers now, always heels.

I love jewellery and have lots of rings but I'm not really into spending a lot on designer clothes. I'm a high-street girl. Topshop's my favourite and, online, I found a random website called Dolls Kill with loads of stuff I like. I'm not all that into fashion, to be honest. If I see something I like, I'll buy it, but I don't follow up on whatever the trend might be. I do love certain designer things but because of how they look, not for the label. I've never been into designer bags that cost thousands. I look at them and think you could get one at Primark for a fiver and no one would know the difference. I love Primark. It's a key place for me at Christmas for finding bits and pieces for presents for my mum and sister. I was in there not long ago and someone said, 'What are *you* doing here?' Why wouldn't I shop there? People sometimes have funny ideas about us, like no one else would wear something once and think they can't wear it again, but when you're in the public eye people expect something different every time they see you. A boy commented on Instagram about a tee-shirt I was wearing, saying, 'I saw you in that the other day. When you going to stop wearing it, you tramp?' I'd worn it twice!

I love tattoos; I've wanted them since I was thirteen. People ask if I'll regret having them when I'm older but I won't, because they're part of my life. I know some people hate them but everyone's different. My ex wasn't sure about me having them and I don't know if it was a rebellious thing but when we broke up I decided to get one. After that I couldn't stop! I've always been scared of needles and when it came to getting the first one done I was shaking and thought I was going to be sick but it didn't hurt at all. It's on my right arm and reads 'Music is the strongest form of magic'. On my wrist I've got 'A tiger never loses sleep over the opinion of sheep', which is about not caring what other people think. I've got the date in Roman numerals when the four of us girls first got together, in August 2011. I got some artwork done on my left arm – 'Once upon a time' – to do with me and Jake, and next to it I've got a feather with an eye that was done by a famous tattooist in New York, Bang Bang. He's done

I'VE GOT THE DATE IN ROMAN NUMERALS WHEN THE FOUR OF US GIRLS FIRST GOT TOGETHER, IN AUGUST 2011.

Rihanna, Katy Perry, Justin Bieber, and it's really hard to get an appointment. I was really lucky because we were working with Justin Bieber's tour manager, in America, and he got me in.

Sometimes when we do an appearance the four of us wear what we want but when it's something big, a special red-carpet event, we have a colour scheme and I love that. It's much stronger. I'm good friends with a designer called Suzanne Neville, who specializes in wedding dresses, and she's made two dresses for me to wear on the red carpet at the Brits. In 2015 she did a proper Jessica Rabbit dress in red, a colour I *love* to wear, with a fishtail. It was amazing, tailored to fit me exactly, and was perfect. I love that style – it's really good for girls with curvy figures. For 2016 our colour scheme was cream and gold, which we'd never done before, and I wanted something fitted and lacy and girly, still in that fishtail style. I tend to stick to black and red so it was really nice to wear something different, and the dress was amazing. Everyone said they could see how I was going to look as a bride! A few years ago I'd never have worn something like that – a lot of it is to do with being confident, as well as the people you surround yourself with. The girls are so positive. It's funny how you always want what you don't have. I might have days when I look at them and think I'd give anything to be that slim, then Jade will look at me and say she wants my curves. The grass is always greener.

LEIGH-ANNE : At the start of Little Mix, we all had our own symbols that summed up our look: I was the one with the hat; Jesy had a boombox and was quite hip-hoppy; Jade had the geek-chic, the bow tie; and Perrie was the Boho one with a little flower. Since then we've all experimented. I've gone from being the one with the

I love Mac products. Whenever we go in one of their stores we spend so much money. We're like kids in a sweet shop. I also like Rimmel, and Sleek contouring products. In 2013 we brought out our own range with Collection, and I loved that. My one tip: if you're having a day when you feel rough, wear a really nice red lip and a pair of sunglasses and you can't go wrong.

I used to have amazing long hair and it got ruined on *The X Factor* with constantly being coloured and having heat on it. My hair is short now and I wear clip-in extensions. I'd never use the glue-in ones, they're so bad for your hair. I've got really curly hair, like ringlets, and I wear it natural. I think people are surprised to see my hair is short. At one time I never used to go out without my extensions in but now it doesn't bother me.

LEIGH-ANNE ★ There's so much pressure on young girls to look perfect. They see stuff on social media and they're thinking, 'Why don't I look like that?' The airbrushing on the pictures is a joke, it's not real, but kids don't know any better. It's so frustrating all this falseness coming across as the way everyone has to look. All of us in Little Mix are different shapes and sizes; we all look completely different. We're not perfect, and we try and get the message through that you don't have to look a certain way, that it's not about how small your waist is or how big your bum is. It's about substance – who you are as a person and the talent you have.

One thing I can say is that I might have some stretch marks and maybe not the flattest stomach, but I love my body. I'm very body-confident. If I'm on holiday, wearing a bikini, I might get scrutinized and there might be nasty comments online but I don't care. I tend not to listen to

negative comments about my looks because the people saying all the bad stuff are probably sat behind their computers, hating their lives, with nothing else to do.

I think everyone has to embrace what they have and that's something we try to get across with inspirational songs. We write from personal experience and our own insecurities come through in the music. Only recently someone we worked with told us about his daughter coming back from school crying because she hated her thick Afro hair and wanted to be like the blonde girls. In his eyes, she was perfect, beautiful, and it broke his heart to see her so unhappy. He did everything in his power to get her to love and appreciate herself the way she was but nothing got through until he played her our song 'Little Me'. It's about believing in yourself – what you'd tell your younger self: 'Tell her to shout out / Talk a bit louder / Be a bit prouder.' That little girl carried the lyrics with her and it changed the way she felt. She went from hating her hair to loving it. We were in tears when he told us. It's incredible to think that by listening to our songs people feel they can be themselves. To touch someone's life like that through our music is the most amazing thing and makes everything worthwhile. I love that people can relate to our lyrics.

I didn't ever think about us being role models, never knew that was going to happen. We just wanted girls to feel better about themselves, to show them that we stick together, no bitching or any of that. We're there for each other. That's what we wanted to come through in our music.

TO TOUCH
SOMEONE'S
LIFE . . . THROUGH
OUR MUSIC IS THE
MOST AMAZING
THING AND MAKES
EVERYTHING
WORTHWHILE.

JESY: I feel like the pressure for young girls to look a certain way is massive. So many have surgery and lip fillers now, and a lot of that is to do with social media. I hate that there's a warped view of how girls should look, that they're supposed to be skinny-hipped and big on top and have huge lips. You see really young girls, even five-year-olds, posting pictures of themselves pouting because they've seen what older girls are doing. You see twelve-year-olds with hair extensions and false eyelashes. When I was that age I didn't even know what make-up was. It's mad, there's so much pressure.

I just think you have to be yourself. You'll never be happy unless you accept who you are. It's what I've learned to do, instead of picking myself apart like I used to. Everybody in the world has stuff about themselves they don't like, even the most beautiful people. I love that everyone's different. If we all looked the same, it would be boring.

I HATE THAT THERE'S A WARPED VIEW OF HOW GIRLS SHOULD LOOK.

If I ever have kids, I want them to grow up getting muddy in the park, climbing trees and doing what kids should be doing, not to get obsessed at a young age with an idea of how they should look, which is massively unrealistic anyway. What about when they're older? They're going to end up hating themselves. It's something all four of us feel strongly about and, in that respect, I feel we're good role models.

The one positive thing I can take from the online bullying that happened to me is that I can share the experience, and though it was a horrible part of my life, hopefully being open about what I went through will help other young girls. It's incredible when we hear that our stories and our music have made an impact. We were working with someone recently whose little girl had been bullied at school because of her hair and the way she looked. She came home distraught, saying she wanted to cut her hair off. It was heartbreaking to think other people had made her feel that way; the bullies had got inside her head. I know exactly how that feels. What finally got through to her was our song 'Little Me', about believing in yourself and not putting yourself down. She really related to it. To know that one of our songs changed that little girl's life for the better is the best feeling in the world.

PERRIE: When I was younger I had a Myspace account with a picture, a profile about the music I liked and that was it. It was a lot more innocent then. Now social media is on a completely different level. It's mental. When I was growing up I found out what I liked and didn't like through experience. Young girls today feel they have to like certain things or look a certain way, wear this and that, because everybody's doing it on Instagram. There are girls who look incredible and have hundreds of thousands of followers on social media, and I think it can make young girls feel bad because they don't look like that. I was a late bloomer in everything. I remember being in the science class when I was thirteen or fourteen and a lad going round pinging every girl's bra strap – I was the only one still wearing a vest. I was fifteen before I realized my friends were shaving their legs. I'd never even thought about it. I'm all for whatever makes you happy but never try to be something you're not. Social media is not real life. The lives it portrays are not the lives that people actually live. I think it's good to be yourself and embrace who you are. That's a lot cooler, in my eyes.

JADE: When you enter this industry you can't hide from what people are saying about you. It's everywhere.

People who don't even know you can be really horrible, laying into you, saying disgusting things.

I never, ever had an issue with my nose until we did an *X Factor* photo shoot for a magazine and they made my nose thinner and pointier in the pictures. It was such a shock. All I could think was, 'What's wrong with my nose? Am I that ugly they had to Photoshop my face?'

It was the first time I'd ever looked at myself like that. They hadn't told me what they were going to do and up until then I'd never even heard of Photoshop, or airbrushing pictures. I was so upset I cried for ages about it. I started hating my nose, thinking I wanted a nose job, and I'd never had that insecurity before. Even now I've got a complex about it. Everyone tells me it's silly, and I know it is, but it's because of what happened. When people say things about our appearance it does affect us. We're normal girls and that kind of criticism is going to hurt.

WHEN YOU ENTER THIS INDUSTRY YOU CAN'T HIDE FROM WHAT PEOPLE ARE SAYING ABOUT YOU.

You have to somehow grow a thick skin, put things into perspective and remember that the majority of people making those comments are insecure and doing it to make themselves feel better. It's always the ones hidden behind a computer screen with an egg for their profile picture that come out with horrible stuff. I think if they can't even show me what they look like, I really shouldn't let their comments about my appearance affect me.

About The Boy

A Different Beat

JESY: On *The X Factor* people had commented about us being normal girls, different shapes and sizes, good role models for kids, and we knew we wanted to write about that. We thought we could maybe inspire kids by being ourselves and not worrying what people think, and we came up with 'Wings'. As soon as we'd written it we knew it would be a single. When we played it to the label I think they were really shocked at what we'd done. It was so exciting, such an anticipated single, everyone wanting to know what our sound would be. When it was released, in August 2012, it went straight to number 1. I remember we were doing a gig with JLS when we found out and we all cried. The fact people were supporting us and loving our music was really exciting. We felt we'd achieved something amazing.

The first album, *DNA*, went into the US chart at number 4, which made it the highest debut for a British girl group since the Spice Girls, in 1996. That was crazy, especially as I really looked up to the Spice Girls when I was younger. Since then we've grown up a bit and our music has evolved, so for the second album, *Salute*, the sound was more R&B. As soon as we finished the *Salute* tour, in 2014, we started working on the third album. We'd been due to do a twenty-date tour in America but it was cancelled so we could concentrate on the album. When we started writing it just wasn't happening, and in the background there was stuff in the magazines about us splitting up, which was stressful. We were in the studio, staying up until four in the morning with producers, writing, thinking we had a single, then taking it to the label and they'd say no. Sometimes you think, 'This is it,' then other people don't like it and you're left asking, 'What am I hearing, then?' It's pressure. After a while we were all thinking, 'Is this ever going to happen? Are we going to get dropped?' We managed to get an album together, took it to the label and sat there listening to it, and all the time I was thinking that I hated it. I cried my eyes out. We're such perfectionists, and it wasn't good enough. I didn't want to do it and the others felt the same. I've never wanted to be the type of artist to bring out an album with only a couple of good tracks, where you're sitting there skipping loads of songs.

A few months later we got a call from the label to say they had our single and they played us 'Black Magic'. It was such a different sound I was wary at first, wondering if it was going to work, but I played it to my mum and she loved it. Everyone loved it. When we released it, in July 2015, it went to number 1 and stayed there for three weeks. You can never really know what people will think so it was amazing when it did so well, such a relief. 'Black Magic' is a really special song for me. So are 'Wings' and 'Change Your Life', the first song we wrote together, about believing in yourself and not letting people put you down. The fans love it and when we perform it on tour it's very emotional. Another big one for me is 'I Won't', the song we wrote with Jess Glynne, because we did it around the time we thought we were going to be dropped and it's about not giving up.

I'VE NEVER WANTED TO BE THE TYPE OF ARTIST TO BRING OUT AN ALBUM WITH ONLY A COUPLE OF GOOD TRACKS.

LEIGH-ANNE ⚹ At the start everything was new to us and we didn't know which direction to go in, we just wanted to release great music. With the first album, *DNA*, we were finding our way, writing together, and it was so much fun. We didn't feel any pressure, we had nothing to live up to; we just loved every second. We knew we wanted to do a song that was cool and uplifting and would inspire people and 'Wings' was perfect. It will always be special for me –

point where we had an album but it didn't feel right and we didn't want to put it out so we decided to scrap the whole thing, which was risky and scary. I remember going in for a meeting with our label and thinking we were going to get dropped but they came up with a whole new concept: to go pop. As soon as we heard 'Black Magic' we knew that was our single. It was catchy, hooky and fun. We were so relieved. We took some time off to relax and get away from it all and as soon as we returned – boom! – we got our mojo back and it all came together.

It was a long process, making the third album, and we pulled each other through all the low points. No matter what, we had each other's backs. *Get Weird* is a lot more mature-sounding, with songs like 'A.D.I.D.A.S. (All Day I Dream About Sex)', but I think we manage to pull it off in a way that's tongue in cheek and not too raunchy. We still have quite a young fan base and want to be able to cater for everyone.

I've got so many favourite Little Mix songs. 'Salute' is such an anthem, empowering and amazing. 'Little Me' has a beautiful message, lovely to sing. I absolutely love 'DNA', 'Wings', 'Secret Love Song' and the lyric in 'Weird People': 'it don't matter who you are, you can be who you wanna be.' 'Boy' from the *Salute* album is another favourite, for the harmonies and the concept – 'Girl, you'll be all right, forget that boy' – and the fact it's a cappella. I think 'Lightning' is incredible – the drop, the lyrics, the harmonies, the middle section, the Latin chant. It's like a piece of art and was my favourite to perform on the *Get Weird* tour. Out of all our songs, 'Love Me or Leave Me' is my favourite. That feeling of being in bed with someone and having an argument and they turn their back on you. There's a line that melts my heart: 'And you're turning away like you hate me / Do you hate me, do you hate me?'

they'd found a single for us, 'Black Magic', written by Camille and another writer, Ed Drewett. We had a listen and even though I loved the song, I wasn't sure it was right for us. Leigh-Anne and Perrie liked it straight away and Jesy wasn't sure. Up until then we'd written on every single, and I think part of me was stubborn and didn't want to admit we should use it.

I played 'Black Magic' to my family and my mam was like, 'I don't know what you're worried about, it's an absolute tune.' The more I listened to it the more I fell in love and became obsessed with it.

Once we had it everything began falling into place. Some of the songs we'd written before started fitting in and we could see we had a really good pop album in the making. When we released 'Black Magic', in July 2015, it took off and went to number 1 for three weeks. We're so thankful to Camille and Ed, and Electric, who produced the song. They saved our skins!

I think the third album took us to another level. 'Black Magic' really broadened our fan base. Even if you're not into our music, you can't deny it's an amazingly catchy pop song. When we performed it on the Brits the reaction was so good, and a lot of people were seeing us for the first time as a really incredible girl group. More people take us seriously now. In the beginning our demographic was little girls and boys, and teens. Now we've got a gay fan base, which is amazing, and we're empowering women as well as young girls. Men are starting to fancy us, which never happened before.

After being away for a year and a half doing the *Get Weird* album we were scared everyone would have forgotten about us, but having that gap was actually the best thing because when we came back with

THE LABEL TOLD US TO GO AWAY FOR CHRISTMAS, TAKE TIME OFF, GET OUR HEADS IN THE RIGHT PLACE AND START AGAIN.

flying – on top of remembering twenty dance routines – that it hits you how much there is to take in. We had four production days in Yorkshire, which were crucial. I remember on the tour bus going up there feeling like I wasn't convinced I knew the show well enough to get on stage and perform it. I was anxious about forgetting routines and doing the quick changes, which are scary. I always think I'm not going to get back on stage on time. We learned from the *Salute* tour not to have strappy shoes or fiddly things like socks – anything that's complicated to get into and do up. You only have a matter of seconds so you literally have to run and get into your next outfit as fast as you can, and all the while there's this man counting down in your ear – 'ten, nine, eight . . .' – which makes you feel under even more pressure. Backstage, the outfits are set out on rails with our names on, zips and fasteners undone, ready for us to get them on super-fast. There's a wardrobe lady, who can help you out if you're struggling, and on *Get Weird* we had a lovely lady, Mary. It's frantic getting changed and back on stage in position, having to look calm and ready to carry on. The worst part is that voice in your ear when you're still doing up your zip or something – 'three, two, one . . .!'

THE OPENING NIGHT ALWAYS FEELS STRESSFUL BECAUSE YOU THINK ABOUT ALL THE THINGS THAT CAN GO WRONG.

You never know how it's going to feel performing in front of an audience because adrenalin kicks in and makes it completely different to what you experience in rehearsal. It's awful. My mouth goes dry and the surge of adrenalin takes my breath away. On *Salute* we did the first two songs and I was so out of breath, adrenalin pumping, I didn't know how I was going to continue. You learn how to pace yourself and maintain your stamina throughout the show.

Jake was there for the opening night of the *Get Weird* tour and stayed on for the next few days. I love it when he's around, he makes me feel at home and I don't have to worry about missing him. I do miss my mum a lot and wish I could get to see more of her. She's such a fan she would come to every date if she didn't have to work.

LEIGH-ANNE ⁑ Being on tour is exciting, the most fun ever. It's the best thing about what we do, getting to see the fans every night, thousands of people singing back to us. But I don't think any of us felt really confident in the run-up to the opening of the *Get Weird* tour in Cardiff. We'd lost rehearsal time working on our Brits performance, so when we began production rehearsals we were nervous but we had four long days in Yorkshire to run through everything, working with the actual set and practising the tricky stuff, like flying – what we call 'gags'. It was definitely the most physically challenging tour we've ever done. We've all got better individually as dancers and singers and wanted to push ourselves as hard as we could. We know what we're capable of and everything we do has to be a certain standard. When we put on a show we want it to be amazing so that people will come back and see us again. We'd done the *Salute* tour in 2014, which was huge for us, a mixture of arenas and theatres, but *Get Weird* was so much bigger, all arenas. For me, the O2 is always special because it's such an iconic place and so many artists have played there. It was incredible to think we sold out two dates and extra special to have my granddad from Jamaica in the audience.

Get Weird was the hardest tour we've ever done and it really took it out of me. We were all so knackered after each show that the next morning all anyone wanted to do was sleep and I found I wasn't getting to the gym. I always feel good after a workout, mentally and physically, so I really missed it. It's important to look after yourself while on the road because if you get ill or your voice goes, you won't be able to give your best in the show. You have to try and eat well and rest, take vitamins, but on the last tour I found I was so shattered I wanted to comfort eat. We had catering and there were always treats and temptations on offer, so I ate what I wanted. Luckily, it didn't affect me but I have an image in my head of how I want to look and after the tour I couldn't wait to get back in the gym.

I love being on tour, on the bus. We've got a sleeping area upstairs at the front with rows of bunks, all with little curtains, so you can go and get your head down, get a bit of privacy if you want it. There's an upstairs lounge with a telly and a big horseshoe-shaped leather sofa, where everyone tends to chill. Downstairs, there's a loo, another lounge area with a TV, a couple more leather sofas, a dining area and a kitchen with a fridge and a kettle. That's crucial for Jade, who can't live without her morning cuppa. Some of the others bring home comforts, like Perrie brought her *Frozen* bedding, and Jade brought teabags and Rich Tea biscuits. It was only when I got on the bus I realized I'd forgotten to bring a blanket. We spend so much time together on the bus it has to feel like home. At the end of the night after a show, we get into onesies or pyjamas and relax with our dancers. It's lovely. What I love about touring in the UK is that our families can come and see us, so that's a bonus. I even had my little dog Harvey on the tour bus for a few days, and Perrie brought her dog, Hachi. It's definitely tiring being on the road but we get days off here and there,

> FOR ME, THE O2 IS ALWAYS SPECIAL BECAUSE IT'S SUCH AN ICONIC PLACE AND SO MANY ARTISTS HAVE PLAYED THERE.

and if we're at a hotel with a spa and there's time, we'll fit in some pampering.

I always get scared about the quick changes in any show. I don't work well under pressure, I buckle easily and get clumsy. All the time you're getting changed there's a voice doing a countdown in your ear and I find that really stressful. I'm likely to do something stupid like have a boot on one foot and a sandal on the other in the heat of trying to get back on stage.

Things sometimes go wrong on stage, like on the first day's soundcheck supporting Demi Lovato on her 2014 Neon Lights arena tour, in America, when something hit me on the back of the head and knocked me down. I was on the floor, totally out of it. At first I thought maybe one of the dancers had caught me with an elbow. I'm definitely the girl who cries wolf so the others weren't sure if I was joking around, but luckily Perrie had seen what happened. There were oversized dolls' houses on the set and a heavy wooden door from one of them had fallen on my head. It hurt so much I was groggy and dizzy and had to sit it out for a while. Luckily, I was fine by the time we had to do the show.

On the opening night of *Get Weird*, at the end of the show we were supposed to drop through the stage on our concealed lifts but they didn't work so we were all standing there waving and saying goodbye for an embarrassing amount of time before we ran off. In one of the shows we did in Nottingham, Perrie's wire didn't work during the opening so the rest of us shot up into the air and she was left stranded on stage. You're always going to have a few of those moments, especially in a complicated show with so much going on. As long as we carry on and don't give it away, I don't think people really notice when things go wrong.

I loved the set for the *Get Weird* tour, the scale of it and all the colours. Depending on the light it was constantly changing and had a crazy, anything-goes feel. We wanted people to come and have that sense of entering a weird and wacky place, and leave feeling on top of the world. I was so excited, although we were all nervous, just because we felt we hadn't had enough rehearsal time. On the opening night, in Cardiff, we felt a bit of pressure and there were a few production issues, but it went well and the crowd was amazing. And we got great reviews.

Newcastle is always emotional for me because my family is there – my mam and dad and brother and my nanna, who doesn't come to watch me that often, and all my friends, so it's a big one. Little Mix have had a lot of support from the North East so it's really nice to go and put on a good show for them.

I still can't get my head round all the thousands of people buying tickets to come and see us. *Get Weird* started out as thirteen shows in the UK and Ireland and kept growing … and growing. In the end, we did thirty-four shows in fifteen different cities! Keeping a show that size on the road means three tour buses, nine trucks, a touring crew of thirty-two working on the lighting, video, audio, rigging, catering, wardrobe, accounting, merchandising, stage set and props, as well as a team behind the scenes working on the show's design, music and video content, and making sure the whole thing goes to plan. The scale of it is hard to take in.

You'd think when we're touring we'd get sick of each other but we love it on the bus. There's a nice atmosphere after the show. We'll sit upstairs in the living area and watch movies and chill. You don't get homesick with good people around you. I always have a few home comforts, like my pillow, my favourite jumper, my onesie and my parka, last thing you ever want to do and if I'd been able to go on and give a good performance, I would have done. I went home, my mum looked after me and all I did was sleep. Sometimes you need the comfort of being in your own bed and a day or two away from work to get better. Luckily, the antibiotics I was on cleared up the infection and I was back on the road again in time for the next date, in Sheffield. We managed to reschedule the Belfast concerts but obviously people were upset, and while I had some lovely get well messages, I got loads of flak as well. I think some people assume you can perform no matter how you're feeling but we're not robots and it's not always possible, however much you might want to.

In September 2015 we were due to perform 'Black Magic' live on *America's Got Talent*, appearing with a gymnastic team called AcroArmy, who'd been on the show the year before. On the day, my shoulder went and I couldn't move. I was in agony, screaming. Part of the routine involved jumping off the stage into the arms of one of the gymnasts and no way was I going to be able to do it. At the same time it was such a big TV appearance for us, the reason we'd flown over there, it was almost like I had to get through it, no matter what. It was a nightmare. I ended up at the doctor being given injections to numb my shoulder and I was in so much pain I was sobbing. He gave me twenty injections and said he couldn't give me any more, but I was still in agony so he sent me for a lie down. It was the most surreal thing. In the bed next to mine was a famous celebrity and we ended up chatting, not really knowing what to say to each other. Awkward! The pain wasn't going away so the doctor said he'd give me more shots but warned me I'd feel as if I was drunk. In the end I had something like fifty injections and my back was smothered in bruises. Before the show, when

I was getting my hair and make-up done, people were feeding me coffee to wake me up. I was so out of it I can't remember anything much about the performance, just that on stage I couldn't get my balance. It was awful, the worst thing I've had to do.

In a normal job you can take a day off and no one has a go at you, whereas in this job if you miss a performance, everyone's writing articles, commenting on social media and throwing abuse at you.

Change Your Life

The End

Perrie

I'd like to think that what we've been through and the success we've had as Little Mix will inspire people who have a dream to really go for it. I'd say be ambitious and at the same time don't expect anything to be handed to you on a plate. A lot of what we've achieved has come through hard work, so be prepared to put in the effort and energy, and be patient. Sometimes it's about timing. You might find that people put you down, but never give up and when something, or someone, knocks you back, keep in mind the bigger picture. What is it you want? How can you get there? Believe in yourself, even if no one else does, and always keep the passion, the fire in your belly. Be the one who proves that the people who didn't believe in you were wrong.

BELIEVE IN YOURSELF, EVEN IF NO ONE ELSE DOES, AND ALWAYS KEEP THE PASSION.

Jesy

I don't think any dream is unrealistic. If there's something you want, a job you dream of doing, go for it. You'll have to work hard, because nothing comes easy, but I genuinely believe if you really want something you can make it happen. It's a lot about what's in your head, believing in yourself. You only live once, and that's why it's important to live your dream. Don't get to the end and realize you didn't enjoy your life because you didn't dare go for the thing that would have made you happy.

DON'T GET TO THE END AND REALIZE YOU DIDN'T ENJOY YOUR LIFE BECAUSE YOU DIDN'T DARE GO FOR THE THING THAT WOULD HAVE MADE YOU HAPPY.

JESY

Fears and phobias: I hate spiders, which is weird because as a child I used to watch a cartoon called *Spider in the Bath* about a friendly spider. Our house in Cornwall was full of spiders and my mum's terrified of them, and I think I picked up on that.

Pet hates: People burping when they're eating their food. Also, I hate that there are gaps in toilet doors in America and people can see you. I don't like snobby people, the ones up their own arses who think they're better than other people. Get over yourself!

Greatest strength: Overcoming how I felt about myself after all the abuse I got and becoming more confident. Not caring what other people think.

Favourite way to unwind: Going home, being in pyjamas or a onesie, no make-up on, watching *TOWIE*, and eating Domino's. Such a chav!

Most treasured possession: I've got a book I made for me and Jake for Christmas 2015, with all the pictures we've taken together, the first text messages we sent each other, ticket stubs from the first movie we went to see. It's like a massive fairy tale book.

One song that's special: 'Tenerife Sea', by Ed Sheeran.

Music icon: Missy Elliott or Beyoncé.

Biggest splurge: I bought Jake a Vivienne Westwood suit for Christmas that cost about £6,000. I'd never spend that much on me but happily spent it on him. He loves it but he made a hole in the trousers in the space of a few months, so that was a good purchase!

What makes you cry: Everything, I'm such a baby. When the other girls are upset, if someone's hurt them. If my family is upset. The film *The Notebook* always makes me cry. Sometimes the girls and Jake make me cry with laughter.

Favourite comfort food: Domino's pepperoni pizza.

Any superstitions: I never used to be superstitious or believe in psychic stuff but when we were promoting 'Black Magic' we met a woman called Anne Jirsch, who does readings for loads of famous people, and everything she told me has come true – like my engagement and my brother having a baby boy.

Ever been starstruck: I was a huge fan of Jessie J before *The X Factor* and I'd booked tickets to see her in concert, then she was at Judges' Houses with Tulisa, so she saw us perform before I saw her. That was my biggest moment.

Something about you that people will find surprising: I wanted to be a sprinter when I was younger and when I was ten I was the fastest runner at 100 metres in my borough. The starting gun frightened me so much I gave it up. I'm still quite fast. I had a race with Jake the other day and beat him.

One special Little Mix moment: Performing at the Brits. I'd wanted to do that for so long.

Believe in fate: I believe everything happens for a reason and that the four of us were meant to be together in Little Mix.

Secret passion: I love badminton. Me and Jake love going to the sports centre down the road from where we live and having a game. We've got our own racquets! We're both competitive but Jake's better than me. He's one of those people who is good at everything.

Can't live without: I couldn't live without the girls or my family, and that includes Jake.

One thing life has taught you: Not to worry about what people think. Life's too short. Sad as it sounds, you are going to die one day, so you have to enjoy life for what it is. At the end of the day you're probably never going to see the people who say nasty things about you and if you let them affect you, you're never going to be happy, so care less about what people think.

Best advice you've been given: To not read negative stuff because it takes over your life and you can't live like that.

Attitude to life: Good. I feel really strong and confident, positive about life and where my career is going. I'm in a really good place.

Leigh-Anne

I never dreamed I would be where I am today, even though it was what I always wanted. It didn't seem possible that such a life-changing thing could happen to me, a normal girl. It goes to show that dreams *do* come true, so you should always work hard, believe in yourself and never lose hope.

DREAMS DO COME TRUE, SO YOU SHOULD ALWAYS WORK HARD, BELIEVE IN YOURSELF AND NEVER LOSE HOPE.

LEIGH-ANNE

Fears and phobias: Flies, daddy-long-legs, moths, wasps – any insects that fly, basically.

Pet hates: London drivers, bags on the table when you're about to eat.

Greatest strength: My compassion.

Favourite way to unwind: On a beach in a tropical place.

One song that's special to you: Usher's 'U Got it Bad'.

Music icon: When I was growing up it was Mariah Carey. Now it's Rihanna. I adore her. Chris Brown too.

Biggest splurge: My Celine bag. It cost £2,500.

What makes you cry: When I'm feeling down about something and someone is kind and asks if I'm OK, I'm gone.

Favourite comfort food: Nachos, freshly made, with pico de gallo and guacamole.

Any superstitions: I wouldn't walk under a ladder.

Ever been starstruck: Every time I see any artists. I've met Rihanna three times and every time I wanted to faint. When Justin Bieber came into our dressing room at the Radio 1 Teen Awards, in 2015, it was a surreal moment. He got us all in a huddle and said a prayer. I couldn't speak.

Something about you that people would find surprising: I used to be a cheerleader in primary school.

One special Little Mix moment: Selling out the O2 on our first arena tour in 2014, singing 'Little Me', and seeing all those people there to see us. I burst into tears. I couldn't believe we'd done it. It was always one of our dreams.

Believe in fate: 100 per cent – that's why we're together.

Secret passion: My fashion blog, leighloves.co.uk

Can't live without: My close family, my circle of friends, my dogs.

One thing life has taught you: Have confidence, believe in yourself, because if you don't, no one else will. If you want something, work hard and you'll get it. I'm living proof.

Best advice you've ever been given: Just to have confidence and believe I am the best so that when I go on stage I know I'm amazing and will deliver.

Attitude to life: Have fun and cherish the important people around you. Never take anyone or anything for granted and always be grateful for what you have.

Jade

My message is to be confident and follow your dreams, however cheesy that might sound. It happened for us and it can happen for you too. Whenever we have a meet and greet we see first-hand the effect our music has – kids who are self-harming or suffering depression saying our songs have helped them. When I was growing up, there weren't any artists I could look up to who made me feel good about myself – like when I went through that whole horrible time at school. I think if there'd been someone I could have listened to and related to back then, it might have made a difference to how I felt, and that's why I think it's important for us to write songs like 'Little Me' and 'Clued Up' that can inspire people. It's important to believe in yourself and persevere. I tried for *The X Factor* three times, even though I had a fear of standing up on stage and being rejected, so go for it, even if you don't get there right away.

DON'T BE THE PERSON WHO LOOKS
BACK AND THINKS, 'WHAT IF?'

JADE

Fears and phobias: Clowns.

Pet hates: Snobs. People who don't put their hand over tiheir mouth when they cough.

Greatest strength: Keeping calm and staying relaxed in stressful situations.

Favourite way to unwind: Lying in bed watching RuPaul's *Drag Race* on TV.

Most treasured possession: I've got a gold and ruby ring I was given when I was about twelve. I never take it off.

One song that's special: Diana Ross's 'When You Tell Me That You Love Me'. It reminds me of my mam.

Music icon: Diana Ross.

Biggest splurge: A holiday for me and my family. We went to Tenerife.

What makes you cry: Missing my family.

Favourite comfort food: Roast dinners. They remind me of home.

Any superstitions: I wouldn't walk under a ladder. And I believe in karma.

Ever been starstruck: All the time, especially with people I grew up listening to, like the Spice Girls. I got really starstruck when we met Dionne Warwick.

Something about you that people will find surprising: I've never burped in my life.

One special Little Mix moment: When we promoted the *DNA* album in America the hype was so huge it really felt special. I remember feeling emotional at the time that we were having such an impact on young girls.

Believe in fate: Yes, 100 per cent. I believe we were meant to be together.

Secret passion: I love art and drawing and painting. Before Little Mix I was going to do an art degree and always think that when I retire I'll have a little studio and paint as a hobby.

Can't live without: Tea and biscuits. I'm addicted. I can't start the day without a cup of tea. My phone as well, because it helps me keep in contact with family and friends.

One thing life has taught you: No matter what I'm going through, however bad I'm feeling, it always gets better. And someone's always got it worse than you, so you have to appreciate what you have.

Best advice you've been given: To enjoy what I'm doing. It's easy to moan and feel sorry for yourself, forget the position you're in, but this kind of job isn't going to be forever so make the most of it while it lasts.

Attitude to life: Just plod along. I think I am a very chilled-out person and very rarely get angry. I've learned to make the most of my time with people I love. You never know what's going to happen.

In loving memory of my Great Auntie Norma 1940–2016. Love you to the moon and back.